HOW
I GOT
HERE

A Memoir

CEIL LUCAS

Book Publishers Network
P.O. Box 2256
Bothell • WA • 98041
Ph • 425-483-3040
www.bookpublishersnetwork.com

10 9 8 7 6 5 4 3 2 1

Printed in the United States of America

LCCN 2017943950
ISBN   978-1-945271-61-8

Editor: Julie Scandora
Cover Designer: Gary Gore
Book Designer: Melissa Vail Coffman
Production: Scott Book

We do not eradicate the early patterns of our experience. They remain with us all of our lives.

— Louis Rubin Jr.

And I fly over the trees and chimneys of my town, over the dockyards, skimming the masts and funnels, . . . over the trees of the everlasting park, . . . over the yellow seashore, and the stone-chasing dogs, and the old men, and the singing sea. The memories of childhood have no order, and no end.

— Dylan Thomas

CONTENTS

PROLOGUE

A FORMER COLLEAGUE ONCE SAID, "I really have no memories before the age of eight." I was simply astounded, could not completely understand how this might be possible. I'm pretty sure that my first memory is from when I was close to two years old. I'm sitting on the cement driveway in the bright sun of a Phoenix morning, and I am turning the handle of a hurdy-gurdy. My pajamas have plastic feet in them. It is early summer of 1953. That was the beginning of my memoried life, and this first memory has hundreds of siblings.

Not only do I have very early memories, but also and more importantly, all my childhood memories have stayed with me, pretty much intact, all through my life. In his book, *Small Craft Advisory*, Louis Rubin says, "We do not ever eradicate the early patterns of our experience. They remain with us all our lives." And, of course, the over-quoted William Faulkner with "the past is never dead. It's not even past." What Rubin and Faulkner were getting at is that our adult lives are inevitably shaped by our early patterns, by our pasts. And those pasts must include those who came before us—in my case, the one who made the decision in 1679 at age forty-nine to leave England and sail to Philadelphia and a new life and the one who left Dundee, Scotland, in 1654 at age twenty to be transported to the Eastern Shore of Maryland.

I have been twenty years old and also forty-nine, so I look at those decisions through my memory of my life at those ages and what a huge decision such as those would have been like. And those who made their way to North Carolina, Pennsylvania, Indiana, Illinois, Oklahoma, and New Mexico.

My father was born in Estancia, New Mexico, in 1909, before New Mexico became a state in 1912; my mother was born in Decatur, Illinois, also in 1909. Both of them had ancestors who had been in

America more than one hundred years before there was an America; both of them had ancestors who moved. And they kept moving after they married in 1935, around the western United States and then to Guatemala City and Italy.

This is a memoir that looks to the past, of course, but not just to the beginnings of my memories in Phoenix in 1953. This memoir also looks to where I came from, as far back as genealogy will let me go. Filling in the genealogical picture has thoroughly shaped how I think about myself. Family lore had it that we were Irish; family stories had it that we were Dutch Protestants. Genealogy tells me that we are English from County Wiltshire—De Lucas in Kent before that—Quakers who chose to leave, and Scots from Fife, prisoners of Cromwell, transported to Maryland's Eastern Shore. This knowledge is as important to how I think about myself as are the memories from my lifetime. Genealogy has given me memories of those who came before me, even ten generations before me, pictures in my mind of the places they left, pictures of where they ended up. Their stories have become mine.

The nutshell summary: I was born in Phoenix in 1951. In 1956, my father the civil engineer, accepted a job in Guatemala City. More about that later. In 1960, he was hired by the Food and Agriculture Organization (FAO) of the United Nations located in Rome, Italy. I came to the United States for college in 1969. I returned to Rome for the 1971-1972 academic year. While I have travelled extensively, I have lived permanently in the United States since August of 1972. Ages five to twenty-one: four years in Guatemala City and twelve in Rome, with two nine-month stints for freshman and sophomore year at Whitman College in Walla Walla, Washington.

"I didn't grow up here," I almost always say when meeting someone for the first time. "I wasn't raised here." "Here" means America, the United States, the States. In my mind, it is crucial for someone meeting me for the first time to know that whatever "here" is about, I have always felt that I am not, nor never will be, totally of it. I have learned it by brief visits across my childhood and from living here since 1972.

Among other things, the meaning of "here" attests to the sheer power of "here" in twenty-first century life, what "America" means and has meant. John Kininmont in 1654 and Robert Lucas in 1679 were also not from here, but it is the single largest irony of my life that now, after 360 years and ten generations on both sides, I really am from here, no denying it. I am American. Those before me were here over a hundred years before there was an American nation to speak of, but John Kinnaman of Stokes County, North Carolina, was here in 1776; Robert and Charles Lucas, both born in Bucks County, Pennsylvania, were here in 1776. Of a total of ten generations, eight were born here.

And so this memoir of my life until age twenty-one is bound by large and sturdy threads—a thread of movement, my own, that of my immediate family, and of ancestors; a thread of genealogy, the story—as clearly as I know it—of those who came before; a thread of language—in truth, I was not bilingual until I was five. Bilingualism first came in 1956 within four or five months of living in Guatemala City. But it is also true that I can't remember a time when I was not bilingual, and I was raised, until the age of eighteen, with many children just like me, bilinguals in English and Spanish or Italian or Greek or French or Portuguese or Arabic or Amharic. . . . Nothing at all unusual; that's just who we were, many of us multilingual. We were just like millions of children around the world being raised multilingually.

But this no doubt accounted for a part of the culture shock that I experienced when I came to the United States for college in the fall of 1969 and was met by classmates almost all of whom had been raised exclusively in English with maybe some Spanish or French courses in high school.

By December of 1960, age nine, I spoke English, Spanish, Italian, and French, all fluently. As an adult, I have added American Sign Language (ASL) and Irish, but the first four set the stage, and I have maintained them, the English and the Italian somewhat more strongly than the French and Spanish. I live every day with six languages in my head, and none is ever not online; they are all always available, just in case—a headful of languages. And, finally, a thread of America—what it meant to be here during the years that it was being formed and which parts of it American parents living abroad, along with teachers and school administrators, chose to try to build an identity as American in their children deeply tempted by other languages and cultures. Some adults didn't try or didn't succeed. A number of my classmates agreed to come back to the United States for college and then returned as soon as they could to the rest of the world for their lives and careers.

But many of us stayed, maintaining contact with the rest of the world as best we have been able to—in my case, through travel, professional work, and the teaching of Italian since 1973. We are Americans, and we are of the world.

This is about how I got here.

THE GUATEMALA YEARS

Carlos and Miguel

I remember clearly the day that I learned the word *pallbearer*. Actually, I can't say that, at age six, I knew the word *assassination*, but it was clear that someone had been killed and Mother said, "Daddy has been called to the presidential palace to serve as a pallbearer."

Some background: 1954 marked the beginning of a very long and turbulent period in the history of Guatemala, a period that in effect lasted until 1996 and the end of the civil war. The story has been told and written about many times. Jacobo Arbenz Guzmán had been democratically elected in 1950 and had the principal mission of restoring to peasants lands that had been appropriated by wealthy landowners and the United Fruit Company (UFCO), which by 1944 owned millions of acres of banana land in Guatemala, mainly along the southern coast.

By 1954, five years before Castro came to power in Cuba, US fears about communism taking root in all of Latin America reached a fever pitch, and Arbenz's land redistribution was perceived as very alarming. The CIA sponsored a covert operation against Arbenz, known as PBSUCCESS. As Stephen Streeter states, " Dulles [John Foster, Secretary of State] and other U.S. officials did not need to be functionaries of United Fruit to see that the Arbenz administration's reforms endangered U.S. interests." Oh, yes, as is well-known, the US government had long had a direct hand in the political affairs of Guatemala. Some say it was because of the deep fear of communism and powerful efforts to keep it from taking hold. Others say that it had to do with the huge US economic interests in Guatemala.

In 1948, the United Fruit Company was the largest employer in the country. It was joined by International Railways of Central America and the power company Empresa Electrica. These kinds of companies had a direct interest in who was running the country, and the

Eisenhower administration—with the director of the CIA Allen Dulles and his brother John Foster Dulles, the secretary of state—was eager to protect these interests. It was probably a combination of both. Actually, this concern with communism spreading had its origins in the Truman Doctrine, announced March 12, 1947, just two years after the end of World War II, a doctrine to stop Soviet expansion in Europe and elsewhere with military and economic aid. The application of the aid started with Greece and Turkey.

La Hora (permission of Guatemala National Archives).

The outcome of the covert operation in Guatemala came to be known as the "Liberation," presumably liberation from Arbenz and possible communism. The CIA had three candidates in mind for the presidency. Juan Córdova Cerna was a coffee farmer and consultant to the United Fruit Company. Streeter states that, according to Howard Hunt—that Howard Hunt, the Watergate one—Córdova Cerna was rejected as a candidate because he had been diagnosed with throat cancer. Streeter goes on to observe that "Córdova Cerna must have recovered from his illness, because between 1953 and 1955 he served as the principal liaison between the Eisenhower administration and Castillo

Armas, the ultimate CIA choice." The second candidate was Miguel Ydígoras Fuentes, a general who "was pro-Nazi until 1943, when he switched his allegiance to the United States." The third candidate was Colonel Carlos Castillo Armas, the illegitimate son of a landowner. He had been Arbenz's classmate at the Guatemalan military academy and had studied at the US Army school in Leavenworth, Kansas, for eight months. In June of 1954, with fortification from the CIA, Castillo Armas and a band of 150 soldiers invaded Guatemala from Honduras. The Guatemalan army refused to defend Arbenz, and he stepped aside. A ruling junta was formed, headed by Elfego Monzón. Castillo Armas succeeded Monzón and was formally declared president on September 1, 1954. He cancelled Decree 900, which had facilitated land reform. The cancellation forced peasants to vacate their newly acquired lands, as a lot of it was reappropriated by the United Fruit Company.

Diario de Centro America (permission of Guatemala National Archives).

At the CIA's request, Castillo Armas also formed the National Committee of Defense Against Communism (Comité de Defensa Nacional Contra Comunismo, CDNCC). Castillo Armas was assassinated by palace guard Vásquez Sánchez on July 26 of 1957. Vásquez Sánchez then evidently committed suicide in an upstairs room of the palace. Even though Vásquez Sánchez's political affiliation has never been confirmed, the *Diario La Hora*'s July 31, 1957, headline proclaimed, "*Con el asesinato de Castillo Armas, el comunismo ha perdido otra batalla.*" (with the assassination of Castillo Armas, communism has lost another battle). The *Diario de Centro America* from the same day stated that "*Comunismo Internacional Autor del Vil Asesinato*" (international Communism the author of the vile assassination).

William A. Lucas (*dark glasses, lower right*) at Castillo Armas's funeral, July 1957 (permission of Guatemala National Archives).

President Eisenhower characterized the death of Castillo Armas in the *Milwaukee Journal*, July 28, 1957, as "a great loss" and states, "Under his leadership the threat of Communist domination of his country was repulsed and Guatemala became a valuable member of the Organization of American States." He sent his son, Major John Eisenhower, to represent him at the funeral.

Following the assassination of Castillo Armas, first presidential designate Arturo González López assumed the presidency. An election was attempted in November of 1957. It was won by Miguel Ortiz Passarelli, the candidate preferred by the Eisenhower government. However,

Passarelli's election was followed by protests in favor of Ydígoras Fuentes, and a second election was eventually scheduled due to accusations of fraud in the first one. Following the election, the Guatemalan Congress voted forty to eighteen to elect Ydígoras president. Secretary of State Dulles warned Ydígoras that "a Guatemalan government with the slightest communist taint would do incalculable harm [to the] U.S. world position." Minister counselor Julio Asensio Wunderlich advised State Department officer Bayard King that "no government could survive in Guatemala unless it was acceptable to the United States Government." Ydígoras Fuentes, with continuing US manipulation, became the next president on February 12 of 1958.

President Miguel Ydígoras Fuentes inspects Nueva Concepción, March 1958; William Lucas is in dark glasses behind the reporter.

That's the background. And into all of this came my father in March of 1956. He worked for the International Development Services, IDS. As Streeter states, "The State Department hired the International Development Services, a nonprofit consulting firm that espoused the department's goal of transforming Guatemala into a land of middle-class farmers. The Castillo Armas administration cooperated by drafting a new agrarian law (Decree 559) that relocated thousands of campesinos to land donated by the United Fruit Company, returned to the Fincas Nacionales (state-owned farms), or acquired through private sale. To help Guatemalan authorities implement the law, the ICA (International Cooperation Administration of the US government) gave the IDS about $10 million for land clearing, access roads, supervised agricultural credit, agricultural extension, irrigation, housing, health facilities, and schools."

My father was a civil engineer who had been hired by IDS to work in Guatemala on irrigation and land development projects. The president of Guatemala when my father arrived in 1956 was Carlos Castillo Armas. In a letter to my mother written in late May of 1956, my father refers to a meeting with Rudolpho (how he spelled Rudolfo) Armas, the president's brother, about an ongoing project, so he clearly had access to the presidential level. His Guatemalan colleagues referred to him as El Ingeniero, the engineer.

A fair amount of time after my father's death in July of 1981, I started thinking about writing this memoir, and in the course of thinking and making notes about what I wanted to talk about, I suddenly asked myself, "Why would an American civil engineer working on irrigation and development projects be summoned to serve as a pallbearer at the funeral of Castillo Armas?" The photo in the July 30, 1957 edition of the *Diario de Centro America* shows him at one end of the casket, wearing sunglasses, looking directly at the camera. And given that his company was a subcontractor to the Department of State, he evidently was serving as one representative of the American government at the funeral. He wasn't just a civil engineer on that day.

In a March 1958 photo, he is standing and looking at Miguel Ydígoras Fuentes, the newly installed president of Guatemala. Ortiz Passarelli had conceded the election, and Ydígoras Fuentes had taken over in January. My father is forty-nine years old in that photo. He is wearing sunglasses and an American-style cotton shirt. The president and his deputy are wearing shirts made of traditional hand-woven cloth, with Mayan symbols on them, long-sleeved in the Guatemalan heat. The president is also wearing a traditional rural hat. He is flanked by a uniformed military officer and is being interviewed by a newspaper reporter with a camera around his neck.

He has come to inspect Nueva Concepción, one of seventeen development zones on the Pacific Slope. It and the zone called La Máquina were the largest, each covering eighty-five thousand acres, the rest ranging in size from fifteen hundred to thirty-one thousand acres. As Streeter states, "The IDS asserted that the U.S. and Guatemalan technical assistance programs had awakened a new sense of community spirit in the zones." In a letter to my mother from June 29, 1956, written after a student riot during which five hundred people marched on the national palace resulting in three students being killed and other students and soldiers being wounded, with a curfew imposed, my father writes, "I feel the government is doing their best for the country and that the strong measures with the hotheads are justified."

But Streeter states, "Conditions in the agrarian zones hardly resembled the rosy picture that U.S. and IDS officials painted: settlers complained about bad roads, insect infestations, insufficient storage facilities, impure water supplies, poor schools, and inadequate medical care."

My father counters, "[Glen] Grisham [the head of IDS] says that we are missionaries."

My father worked for IDS until the late spring of 1960, when he was offered a position at the Food and Agricultural Organization of the United Nations in Rome, Italy. So we lived in Guatemala for almost four years, August of 1956 until late May of 1960. I was five when we arrived and had just turned nine when we left. As an adult, long after we had lived in Guatemala, I have learned all about what was going on politically and socially while we lived there.

Learning the political and economic history as an adult has made me feel as if I had lived in a basement for four years. A lovely basement, to be sure, with a wonderful school, a very safe comfortable house, birthday parties with cake and presents, colorful religious processions, trips around the country, trips to the beach with its black volcanic sand, astonishing Christmas markets, Easter celebrations, airplane trips to the United States, toys, dolls, books, a beautiful blue bicycle, a guppy in a bowl on the nightstand, a remarkable middle-class childhood. And in the house above me, while I could hear feet walking on the floorboards and muffled voices, I, of course, had no way of knowing or understanding the extent of the involvement of the US government in Guatemalan affairs, the depth of the manipulation and control being exerted by American politicians and diplomats, and the powerful impact that this manipulation and control had on the lives of ordinary Guatemalans, who were not members of the tiny elite.

The impact got progressively worse between 1960 and 1996, a period of civil war in which hundreds of thousands of indigenous people were killed and disappeared as they and their opinions were deemed to be obstacles to implementing the government's vision.

As an adult, I have been able to make my way up the stairs from the basement and to take a hard look at what was going on, to see whose footsteps and voices I was hearing. I know now that those footsteps and voices included my father's, and I now have a very clear understanding of what pallbearer means. What strikes me is the sharp contrast between the basement and the upstairs. And I was certainly not alone in the basement. I was joined by the children of USAID employees and of the employees of the American embassy and of various private companies. In a letter to my mother in April of 1956, very soon after he arrived by himself to start working, my father exclaims that there are "over 5000 Americans in the city!" most of them with dependent children who needed schooling.

When we moved to Rome, I was able to come out of the basement for good. The CIA certainly involved itself in Italian politics, most notably in the 1948 elections (and indeed, through 1972), strongly supporting the Christian Democratic party (La Democrazia Cristiana) as a bulwark against the Italian Communist party and the Soviet Union as the Cold War got underway. We lived in Rome, but my father's work for the United Nations took him to most of the countries in South America, parts of West Africa, Korea. My father worked for the United Nations and was less directly involved in the carryings-on of the US government.

As far as I know.

The Rubio's Place

In August of 1956, my mother and I flew to Guatemala City from Phoenix to join my father. He had been working there since April. I was five years old, and I did not start school until January 1, 1957.

The first place we lived in Guatemala City, between August and October of 1956 was the Cielito Lindo apartment building, 7 Avenida and 17 Calle, right in the middle of downtown and near the central produce market and the Panamerican Hotel.

It was a temporary arrangement that my father and one of his colleagues had made. In a letter written April 8 to my mother, my father says, "The housing situation is pretty bad and rents are high as there are over 5000 Americans in the city and many of them get their housing paid." In an early June letter, he provides a sketch of the apartment—two bedrooms, a living room, kitchen, combined hall and dining room, and a bathroom. Windows run the length of the apartment and look out on 17 Calle. "The biggest apartment house in the city," he states, interestingly misspelling its name as "El Ceilito," with the *i* and *e* reversed. It means "the endearing sky," with the Central American Spanish diminutive suffix of endearment, *-ito* (as in *cafecito, platito*). My own name, spelled C-e-i-l, quite naturally became Cielito fairly soon after we arrived. It stayed that way until we moved to Rome in September of 1960, at which point it became the Italian word for sky, Cielo, with the Roman pronunciation in which the initial *ch* becomes *sh*, so it sounded like "shelow." I can count on two hands the number of Roman friends who still call me that, people I have known since 1960 and their children and grandchildren.

Cielito Lindo apartment building in Guatemala City, 2003.

The rainy season in Guatemala runs from mid-May to mid-October, and I remember many rainy mornings during the three months we stayed in this apartment. I remember leaning my elbows on a folded towel to protect them from the rough cement of the windowsill as I stood on a chair and watched the goings-on in the street, absorbing many new sounds and sights and smells. People going to market, many of them with large bundles on their heads, 1950-style cars filling up the street, the sound of conversation and laughter in a language that I did not yet understand, the sight of the surrounding buildings and store awnings. The smell of smoke from fires cooking food in the market and on the street—roasting corn and a thick, hot corn drink, *atol de elote*, and grilled chicken. The smell of car exhaust and of rain.

It was in the central market that I was first saw deaf people. A group of indigenous people in their traditional outfits were sitting on a blanket at the entrance to the market, selling their goods and signing away. Their mouths were not moving, and there was no sound coming from them, just moving hands and active faces. This image would come back to me some thirty-six years later as I started to learn American Sign Language. I wonder now how big the community was, whether the signing differed from community to community, whether the hearing children in the group served as interpreters. A small commissary had been set up by some other American residents, one room on the ground floor of a nearby building. My father mentions going there to buy "pancake flour, syrup, jam, cereal and so on to help out our meals." And Camel cigarettes, of course, no filter. I would accompany my mother there to buy "Yankee" stuff: peanut butter, Kraft mayonnaise in a jar, Hershey chocolate bars. The apartment building is still standing, and an Italian eatery now promises "Pizza, pizza, pizza!"

On a trip to Guatemala in 1990, I made time to go to the central market by myself. I wandered through the aisles, taking in the very familiar sights and sounds and smells. I gradually became aware that my face was completely wet. I was crying. The market had reached in and shaken awake thirty-year-old memories and moved me like an evocative piece of music or poetry. I have never experienced that at any other time in my life.

We then moved, and our home in Guatemala City for October 1956 until October of 1957 was a rented apartment. It was the whole second floor of the house owned by my father's colleague, Rodolfo Rubio. The house looked like a block of cement with windows. A staircase curved up from the downstairs into an open area off which branched a living room, two bedrooms, a bathroom, and a kitchen. Off the open area was a fairly large whitewashed rooftop terrace where the laundry was hung, lush tropical trees in the background. All the rooms had windows, and one of the bedrooms had a small balcony that looked onto the driveway and the unpaved street below. The house was brand new in 1956 and has been added onto since. We didn't have our own furniture; the apartment was furnished very simply. At the top of the stairs was a long, rectangular container for plants that lushly spilled out on both sides. Wonderful aromas of Guatemalan food—tortillas, black beans, chicken—would regularly waft up the stairs. Rodolfo lived with his wife, Elma, two children, Rodolfo and Eugenia, and his aging widowed mother, Doña Chayo. Well, aging in my eyes at the time—my own parents were forty-six when we moved, close in age to the Rubios. Doña Chayo was probably not yet seventy, but she seemed old to me. This was a middle-class house with indoor plumbing, electric lights, kitchen appliances.

Ceil with Mother and Dad in front of the Rubio's place, 1957.

The Rubios' place, 1957.

For Christmas of 1956, Doña Chayo handmade elegant Christmas ornaments out of straw. For Easter 1957, she emptied the contents of fresh eggs into a bowl and later used them for cooking. The eggshells were then filled with confetti and given a glued-on tissue paper lid and painted in bright colors. On Easter Sunday, children and adults laughed delightedly while ambushing each other and cracking the eggs on each other's heads, as the confetti flowed onto our hair and clothes. Very labor intensive for a fifteen-second diversion.

In 1957, the volcano Fuego erupted at night. The volcano overlooks the city. We raced in the car up the highway opposite the volcano to watch the lava flow. For the next three mornings, the rooftop terrace was covered with ash that descended softly and silently like snow.

My mother's father, Buren Oscar Kinnaman, had been widowed in February of 1956, before we moved to Guatemala in August. He and Bess Wallace had married in 1907, but now he found himself alone after forty-nine years of marriage. One of his two sons still lived in Illinois, while he worked in Seattle. And his daughter had decamped to Guatemala City with her husband and daughter. His father was Pleasant Columbus Kinnaman, Indiana born and bred, but Buren had chosen to move west to Decatur, Illinois. He had worked as a mailman on the Illinois railroads, providing a good living for his family even through the years of the Depression. He watched the century change at age sixteen.

And now, at age seventy-three, he was alone and had decided to venture to Guatemala City.

This was without doubt the first time he had owned a passport and probably the first time he had left the United States. And it was one of the only times that I spent any time with him. We showed him the sights of Guatemala—Antigua, the port of San José.

Ceil with Burren Oscar Kinnaman, January 1957.

In the photo, we are standing on the whitewashed terrace of the apartment. He is a man of his era, always with a hat when leaving the house, even to just step out on the terrace. And he has the long and lean Kinnaman look that I see in my mother's face and in the faces of my male cousins. I am almost six and ready to ride.

Ceil with Little Lulu piñata, 1957.

Throughout my childhood, my mother became an expert at melding aspects of Guatemalan and Italian culture with American values and experiences that she wanted to make sure made it into my developing consciousness. My sixth birthday in March of 1957 was no exception.

The photo shows me on the morning of March 19 standing on the whitewashed terrace of the Rubios' place with a piñata of Little Lulu. My outfit is a cross-cultural mix: a Guatemalan woven shirt, red dungarees rolled up, socks, and the ubiquitous black-and-white saddle shoes. I am arm in arm with Lulu, who is a whole head taller than I, enormous by piñata standards. She is seemingly unaware of her violent fate.

Piñatas were, of course, standard issue for birthday celebrations in Guatemala, but where in the city my mother would have managed to find a Little Lulu one is a mystery. I knew about Little Lulu from American funny papers that we had read in Phoenix. Perhaps she appeared in the Guatemalan funny papers as well. She was evidently a representative of American values that my mother wanted to reinforce in this child who was very quickly learning to speak Spanish with a Guatemalan accent.

Little Lulu, alas, was taken to a birthday party at the school and, at the appropriate moment, relieved of the cellophane-wrapped hard candies waiting in a ceramic pot in her belly. She was hung from a rope, and blind-folded children squealed with delight as they aimed a stick at her. I was right in there swinging.

Alfonso (20-19 Avenida A)

What I would like to be able to report is something that he said—a particular conversation, a funny sentence, a laugh. But not only can I not remember any particular sentences or conversations; I also have no memory even of the sound of his voice. We must have spoken Spanish, because he did not speak English, and I didn't speak his native language. I can talk about what he looked like and where he lived. In the only photo I have, he is standing in front of the very small dwelling he lived in with his mother and his younger brother and sister.

His house stands on an undeveloped lot in Guatemala City that would be the future site of a subdivision. Señor Lorenz is our landlord, and he allows Alfonso's family to install their brick house on the lot, no mortar. It is 1957. I know him only as Alfonso—I don't think I ever knew his last name. He is a head taller than I, and his skin is brown. He has jet-black hair and a broad inviting face. His family has come down from the highlands of Guatemala to the city, in hopes of better circumstances.

Alfonso and his family, 1960.

One windowless room of the house contains two narrow, makeshift beds; a crate between them serves as a table. The floor is dirt, packed tight from the weight and traffic of human feet. Next to this room is a cooking area with three walls and space for one person to stand. In this space, his mother tends an open wood fire for a good part of each day and supports herself, Alfonso, and his siblings by making tortillas, which Alfonso delivers to families in the neighborhood, including mine, for the noon meal. The process starts by taking the corn to the market every morning to be ground into mush. When it rains, there is a powerful smell of damp earth mixed with the aroma of wood smoke coming from the cooking fire. There is nothing at all that could be called an amenity—no electric lights, indoor plumbing, running water. Bathing involves a large aluminum tub and a hose that extends over the landlord's wall. No toilet, no sink; the few dishes are washed by hand in a large enamel bowl. This is in sharp contrast to the house across the road that I go home to every evening. From the Rubios' second-floor apartment, we moved to 20-19 Avenida A, still in Zone 10. Ours is the second house completed in what would become a collection of five or six in the subdivision.

The house is spread out on one floor and has a small front yard enclosed by a low cement wall, wide enough on top for small children and dogs to sit on. The street in front of the house is as yet unpaved, packed dirt.

The house itself is long and low, extending on the front from a bedroom and bathroom through an entryway with a fireplace (this in a tropical climate that stays pretty consistently at 80 degrees Fahrenheit), a combined living room and dining room, a kitchen, a utility room, and a covered garage with space for one car.

Off the kitchen is a small bedroom and bathroom for a maid, part of the forethought that went into the planning of this house. The way to the bedrooms is separated from the living room by three low steps that extend dramatically across the space, so one can make a theatrical entrance from the bedroom area into the living room, if needed.

The windows in the living room consist of ten vertical slits separated from each other by plaster dividers set at an angle to the wall. The overall statement made by the public part of the house, and really by the whole house, is modern, late-1950s, American prosperity. Certainly not the colonial adobe and timber and lush bougainvillea statement being made by many of the houses in Guatemala City. Two more bedrooms complete the back of the house, along with a small indoor courtyard open to the sky and a tiny windowless sitting room with a huge cabinet television in it. The television spends its time as a piece of furniture; I have no memory of ever watching it.

House at 20-19 Avenida A, second floor added after May 1960.

And we have amenities: indoor plumbing with toilets, sinks, and a tub, electric lights at any time of the day or night, a refrigerator and a gas stove, a radio. These amenities are not remarkable for 1957 America and were becoming less so in 1957 Guatemala City—but they are re-markable to me as I compare them to Alfonso's living situation. It is to those amenities that I return every day when called for dinner.

Alfonso and I play together after I get home from school, for three years. It strikes me that I was never forbidden to play with him; noth-ing was ever said. An American girl, Kathy Longan, lives on the street parallel to ours, and I could play with her after school, but that never occurs to me. Alfonso doesn't go to school. He spends his days helping his mother, getting the corn for the tortillas ground at the nearby mill, and carrying the tortillas around the neighborhood.

We spend a great deal of time exploring the area around our houses. We discover some abandoned sewage pipes made of brick, wide enough in diameter for a child to wiggle into. We crawl into them and follow them until we come out at a broken spot. At the boundary of the sub-division is a high wall on the other side of which is another collection of houses. Eucalyptus trees and medlar trees heavy with their smooth yellow fruit grow along the wall. We climb the great wide limbs of the eucalyptus, learning quickly that the smooth bark will impatiently push us off to the ground. We climb the fruit trees and sit on the branches stuffing ourselves with fruit, spitting the large brown seeds as far as we can. Some afternoons, we sit on Lorenz's whitewashed wall, peeling and eating small tart oranges or chewing on sugarcane until our jaws ache, juice running down our chins.

Alfonso finds out that a group of prostitutes and their clients gather in a spot somewhat beyond the abandoned sewer pipes. At age six or seven, I have no idea what prostitutes do. My parents of course have a very clear understanding and expressly forbid me to go to that area. Alfonso and I go anyway. I remember that not many prostitutes or clients had gathered on that particular day, but I also realize that I am farther away from my house than I have ever been without my parents. I am also out later than usual. Most days, I'm home well before my father gets home from work and certainly before dusk. I notice a fluttering sensation in my stomach and a feeling that my shoulders are not covered.

Christmas at 20-19 Avenida A, 1957.

As we make our way back to our respective houses, I suddenly become aware of my father running toward me, yelling. He is still dressed in his work clothes and his tie flaps back over his shoulder like a despondent flag. He is forty-eight years old, and his hair is already almost completely white. Apparently the maid and my mother have informed him of my absence, and his anger and concern bring him flying into the street. The direction from which Alfonso and I are coming betrays where we had been. "We tell you never to go there, and yet you won't mind!" he screams.

Alfonso sees that I'm in deep trouble and wisely peels off toward his shack. I somehow manage to elude capture and run into the house and into the safety of my bedroom with its locked door.

"You'll stay in your room until you are sorry!" says my mother. I stay in my room reading until it is time for dinner. I am not at all sorry, but we do not visit the prostitutes again.

Alfonso does not wear shoes. He doesn't even own a pair. One Saturday, my father decides that Alfonso should be taken to buy shoes. Alfonso also does not ride in a car very often. He and I climb into the back seat of the white German Borgwardt while my parents get in the front. Alfonso is barefoot.

Buying shoes means going to the downtown area, very busy on a Saturday morning. Narrow streets are made narrower by the high curbs and wide grey sidewalks on which a variety of vendors set up their wares—corn on the cob, cooked on the spot, tortillas, pots of atol de elote, grilled chicken, lottery tickets, newspapers. A powerful mix of cooking food and car exhaust meet the nose, and music blares out of transistor radios. Signs stick out from the two-story buildings, giving the streets that look of a very colorful and noisy tunnel. And in one of these buildings, on the ground floor, is the shoe store. My father, of course, has in mind exactly what he wants. The salesman disappears into the storeroom and reappears with several shoeboxes. He sits in front of Alfonso and tries various pairs of shoes on his wide and dusty feet. Black, brown, all with laces. No socks. He encourages Alfonso to walk around the store to see how the shoes feel. A pair is finally decided on and paid for, and Alfonso leaves the store wearing the shoes and proudly carrying the box under this arm. We then drive home. Alfonso wears the shoes home to show his mother, takes them off, wraps them in the tissue they had come with, puts them in the box, stores them under the bed, and puts them on again, as far as I know, only for the taking of the photo.

We left Guatemala City in the late spring of 1960. But Alfonso and his family had been forced to find new quarters before we left as the building of the other houses in the subdivision proceeded. One day, I came home from school, and the brick shack was simply gone. I was told that Alfonso and his family had moved up the road, no details. I came to know the construction workers who now started building the rest of the houses in the subdivision and would chat with them after school. One had a condition that caused him to throw up almost every day. As I figured out as an adult, he was a blue-collar worker with no health insurance and certainly could not afford to lose this job, so he dealt with it as best he could.

If he is still alive, Alfonso would be sixty-five or sixty-six. I am certain that I will never see Alfonso again in my life, and we wouldn't recognize each other if we did happen to meet. And I can't talk about the sound of his voice. I can talk about the power of that early and deep friendship in shaping my approach to life and people. I feel very fortunate to have been handed a very early lesson about the nature of having and not having and about, when push comes to shove, what is really important.

Over the course of the years since we last saw each other, I have sometimes forgotten the details of the lesson and have gotten my priorities tangled. But it is true that I am consistently impatient with material and social pretensions, an impatience clearly born from my friendship with Alfonso. I have carried the memory of that friendship tucked under my arm for my whole life, like the little wicker lunch basket that I took with me to school. When unreasonable complaints are voiced about the inadequacy of housing or the quality of food or the lack of amenities, I instinctively pull my arm in to feel the jagged texture of the wicker against my skin.

Evelyn Rogers

I interviewed Evelyn Rogers in Guatemala City in 2003, when she was seventy-eight years old.

I remark, "And I mean, you have to know that in—I mean, in the mid-1950s in the United States, there was no such thing as bilingual education."

Evelyn says, "Of course not."

Ceil: "And what—did you experience—did people give you a bad time about that or wonder what the hell you were doing or . . . ?"

Evelyn: "Not really."

Ceil: "They just . . ."

Evelyn: "Some Americans did. They didn't think it was right."

Ceil: "They all wanted English?"

Evelyn: "All in English. And I said, 'No, because in this world, you're gonna need languages.'"

That was Evelyn Rogers, who founded the eponymous school in Guatemala City in 1948, the Colegio Evelyn Rogers. She was not satisfied with the schools available to her children in Guatemala City and decided to do something about it.

Her father was Alfred Clark, a Virginian who had been sent to Guatemala to build railroads. Her mother was first-generation Guatemalan of Colombian background.

Evelyn was born in Paris in 1925 and lived her first six years in Guatemala and was then sent to a boarding school in Yonkers, New York, and then on to New Orleans, and eventually, Vassar. She returned to Guatemala in 1946 to tend to her dying mother and never left.

The school was organized around the Calvert system, originated in 1905 in Baltimore by Virgil Hillyer. He was headmaster of the Calvert Day School, founded in 1897. It is school in a box, a home-schooling system with curricula and instructional materials now provided to students in over fifty countries.

Evelyn Rogers, age seventy-eight, 2003.

A Child's History of the World, written by Hillyer in 1924, remains a classic. I read it in 1960, before moving to Rome, Italy. It set the stage for the classical world I was about to enter, along with Edith Hamilton's 1942 *Mythology.* Evelyn adopted the curriculum in part because many of the students in the school were Americans, children of State Department and American embassy employees and employees of private companies, like my father. These were children who would no doubt return to the United States for high school and college and needed to be prepared for American school systems.

Parenthetically, I say "Evelyn" and not "Mrs. Rogers," as we were explicitly instructed to address all faculty and staff by their first names. A wonderful practice that caused consternation and confusion in the schools that we all attended after Evelyn's.

Evelyn's significant twist on the Calvert curriculum was to provide as much exposure to different languages as possible, starting in kindergarten. She herself had been raised bilingually in English and Spanish and spoke French. Her view was, as she said, "In this world, you're gonna need languages." This had been her approach since the school was founded. In addition to the basic bilingualism of the school in English and Spanish, we learned French and German, and in later years, she hired a Russian teacher.

This at a time when bilingual education was simply unimaginable in American elementary schools. There had been German-language schools before World War I in Ohio, Iowa, and Nebraska, but most language instruction in American schools between 1919 and the late 1960s had been relegated to high school, two years' worth of classes that routinely left the students thoroughly frustrated and incompetent in whatever language was being required.

Formal attention to bilingual education finally came at the end of the 1960s in Dade County, Florida, and in the early 1970s in San Francisco, in response to the demands of Spanish-speaking and Chinese-speaking parents and communities, so not at all a voluntary endeavor. And there was, of course, always the refrain of the recalcitrant: "My grandparents came from [insert country name], didn't speak English, and learned by being thrown into English schools, by God!"

But with Evelyn, we had languages. I learned to read simultaneously in Spanish and English. In first grade, we were given mimeographed worksheets with drawings of fruits, animals, and household objects that we were to color appropriately and write the name of the item—árbol, *pájaro*, *mesa*, *cama*—tree, bird, table, bed—and we slowly moved on to actual texts in both languages. In an exception to the policy on terms of address, we called our French teacher Madame. Fairly quickly, she renamed me "Ceil La Bavarde"—Ceil the Chatterer, reminiscent of French medieval kings such as Clovis II le Fainéant (Clovis II the Lazy) or Pepin le Bref (Pepin the Short)—since I was evidently quite enthusiastic about talking in class. German classes started a bit later.

On the playground, we unconsciously alternated between Spanish and English. We had spoken English at home in Phoenix between 1951 and the move to Guatemala in August of 1956, with no exposure to other languages at all. January 1, 1957, the first day of school in Guatemala City, marked the beginning of intense exposure to other languages and cultures and of my lifelong and continuing love affair with language.

One of the highlights of school at Evelyn's was the field trips we were taken on to local companies and plants—the Coca Cola bottling company, a chicken processing plant where we observed the doomed chickens hanging upside down, moving along a belt carrying them to their death in boiled water, and a paper products company where we all came away proudly clutching a souvenir sanitary napkin wrapped in colorful paper.

Evelyn also decided that the students needed to learn to swim. She made arrangements with a country club in the city for us to use the pool. Now, the first thing to imagine is the concept of a country club in 1956 in Guatemala City where deep poverty was very easily visible every day. The members of the club would have been the small Guatemalan elite and expatriates working in the country. It had beautifully tended lawns and a gleaming clubhouse surrounded by lush Central American vegetation. The pool was situated in the middle of one of the lawns. It had very narrow cement borders around it, so it seemed to simply appear from under the ground. The water was dark green.

The group of students from the school trooped to the pool at midday in their swimsuits, accompanied by some of the parents, including my mother. The swim teacher was a young Swiss man, Hans Peters, who put zinc oxide cream on his nose to prevent sunburn. We always called him "Profe," from "professor."

Before the lesson started, my mother approached him and said, "Please watch her. She will walk to the deep end of the pool and jump in, and you will think that she knows what she's doing. But she has never been in a pool before."

And that's exactly what I did.

Luckily, the teacher had listened to my mother and fished me out by the back of my suit before I got too far. Following a stern talking-to, the lesson proceeded uneventfully. I was a bit confused because my understanding was that we were there to swim, and that was my plan.

I'm not sure why I have always been pretty fearless. It may come from being the youngest child by twelve years and sensing the relative letting go that my parents did. They had already parented two kids and were a lot more relaxed with me.

It might come from their reinforcement, mostly from my mother, that I could do anything I wanted to do. My father helpfully contributed with "girls can't do math," as he worked on word problems with me. Luckily, I had shown clear aptitude with language, so my pitiful SAT math scores were allowed to slide. Whatever the source of the fearlessness, the swimming lesson was emblematic: This is the assigned task; let's do it.

My parents had indeed wondered whether it was a good decision to take a five-year-old to Guatemala. In a June 11, 1956, letter to my mother, my father says, "I am still not sure we should take Little Toad out of her backyard so Daddy can work in Guatemala."

My mother later told me that they ended up looking at each other, taking a deep breath, and saying, "Well, she'll start school in Guatemala."

One of the very best decisions they ever made. The decision to give me a blue bicycle for Christmas 1959 was excellent, but this was better.

Little Toad (age three) in the sandbox, 1954.

The day is January 1, 1957. I am five years old. The location is Guatemala City, Zone 10, south end of the city. That's the area not far from the Aurora airport. It's a residential area with many tall trees and lots of bougainvillea hanging lushly over the whitewashed walls that surround nearly every house. Broad sidewalks. A quiet area.

The school is a large white mansion that doubles as Evelyn's residence. The building has a covered area in the back with great cement laundry tubs where Indian women wash the sheets and clothing by hand. On the side of the house towards the front is an enclosed porch that serves as the classroom for the first graders. On the opposite side of the front of the house is a row of classrooms that open to the front. The roof of this row of classrooms is thatched. There is a large yard in front of the house with huge cedar trees standing guard. The yard has a swing and jungle bars. It is here that I arrive with my father on the first day of school, probably at 8:30 a.m.

First day of school, January 1, 1957.

We enter at the back of the house, near the laundry room. Even though the walk from our house is not long, we drive in the car since my father is on his way to work. He is dressed in a suit, and I am wearing a dress, socks, and shoes with laces, and my hair is braided. We are holding hands. I carry a plastic bottle with boiled water in it and, somewhat inexplicably, a folder for papers. And suddenly, I am informed that he will be leaving now, that I will be staying for school and he will be going on to work. This comes as a huge shock, as I had imagined that he would be staying with me. Though he had left before for various trips, there had always been an adult staying behind with me. I burst into tears and cry very hard as I absorb the reality that he will be walking away. The adults who are there are obviously ready for this and walk with me into the first grade classroom. The feeling in my stomach at that moment of separation is as fresh now as it was almost sixty years ago.

On our very last night in Guatemala City, we had, of course, moved out of our house and were staying with some friends. Around 8 p.m. there was a knock on the door. It was Evelyn, and she had come to say a final good-bye. She had brought with her a small pin in the shape of a red-and-yellow ladybug. It was for me to wear on a shirt or on my coat, a going-away gift. It was a lovely gesture and a very difficult good-bye.

I would not speak to her again until 1990. I didn't know it yet, but she had gotten me started on the path of being a teacher, and I was fully into it by the next time we made contact. I interviewed her in 2003, but my actual goal on that trip back to Guatemala City was to say thank you for such an amazing start in school, thank you for showing me what I could do with my life. My visit was just in time, as she passed the very next year.

Fourth grade class, spring 1960.

Colegio Evelyn Rogers, Guatemala, late 1950s.

Teaching the Dolls

At some point in mid-1957, I noticed that my dolls were not actually communicating that well among themselves. I was six years old and had a variety of dolls. I had two that were clearly Guatemalan, Juan and María, dressed in traditional clothing, *el traje típico*. There was a Mexican puppet, also in traditional clothing, and a conventional American baby doll, plump, dressed in baby clothes and with brown hair painted on her plastic head. Another girl doll with blond hair wore a flowered party dress and spent most of her time with two small stuffed bears.

Now, they all talked to me just fine, recounting what had gone on during the day while I was away at school. But they did not converse well with each other, and I slowly realized the source of the problem: Juan and María spoke Spanish and a Mayan language—maybe K'iche' or Mam, and the puppet spoke only Mexican Spanish. The baby doll, the blonde, and one of the bears spoke only English. One of the bears was bilingual but not that anxious to take on the responsibility of being an interpreter.

It was clear that I would have to start language lessons, English to the Spanish speakers and Spanish to the English speakers. I began right away, gathering them around me in a semi-circle on my bedroom floor as soon as I got home from school almost every day. Each group had pronunciation drills and spelling tests. On small pieces of paper, I wrote out lists of words that I had dictated to them, one paper for each student. I would include spelling mistakes in the lists, which I would correct with dramatic red checks or circles. Since I was the only child in the house, my mother would quietly peek into the room to see whom in the world I could possibly be talking to.

When we moved to Rome, Italian entered the picture, but the language lessons were slowly replaced by many other activities and interests. And I didn't think about them again until August of 1973. I had moved to

Austin, Texas, to live with the man who would become my husband. He was in the theatre MFA program at the University of Texas. The only job I could find was at the Austin State Hospital, the public mental hospital of the area. With no experience or educational background whatsoever, I was put in charge of recreational therapy on the Harris County ward, the county of Houston, and its surroundings. Patients ranged from those hospitalized with mild depression to severely paranoid schizophrenics, and it was my job to find some unified way to entertain them. We painted while listening to music. I organized a weekly newspaper to which everyone contributed stories varying in their level of coherence and command of English.

But I was twenty-two years old, held a BA in French and art history from Whitman College in Walla Walla, Washington, and was thoroughly unsuited for the field of mental health. A friend of my husband's said, "We hear that your wife speaks French and Italian. Would she be interested in teaching at the university?" This entailed being enrolled in the graduate school, which I did, and I began teaching Italian that fall, the 1973–1974 academic year. I alternated Italian and French through May of 1975, taught during the summers, and continued in various venues after moving to Washington, DC, in August of 1975.

A moment of change came on my very first day of teaching in August of 1973. I was exhausted. I went home and fell face first onto the bed for a long nap. But more important, I was totally in love. It had never quite occurred to me that people actually made a living teaching language but now it did, and I realized that this is quite simply what I wanted to do for the rest of my life. I loved sharing language with the students; I loved watching the lights come on as their skills developed—and I still do. I became a professor of linguistics and focused on the structure and use of the sign languages used by deaf people. After more than forty years of teaching Italian in various places, I don't see myself stopping.

Once, during a lecture to graduate students about the acquisition of sign languages, I remembered about teaching the dolls in Guatemala and Italy. This led to a class discussion as to whether the dolls and action figures of deaf children were hearing or deaf and whether deaf children signed or talked to them. The memory made me sit down. I realized that on the job application at the University of Texas in the part where it inquired about any previous teaching experience, I should not have said, "None." I should have said, "Yes, ages five through nine in Guatemala."

Church, Part I

In letters written to my mother in April of 1956, my father talks about going to church. That would be the Union Church, located at the Plazuela España, just off Avenida La Reforma, a major thoroughfare. The building was dedicated on May 27, 1951, and is still there.

A pamphlet entitled *The Brief History of the Union Church of Guatemala* states that "the origins of our church go back to 1882, the year President Justo Rufino Barrios invited Presbyterians to begin mission work in Guatemala."

In 1943, Dr. Wallace J. Anderson became the first formal pastor. According to *The Brief History*, "His mission sent him to Guatemala. Not able to speak Spanish, he was assigned part time to the pastorate of the English-speaking congregation. This was just what was needed to bring together the various Protestant English-speaking elements into the formal organization of the Union Church of Guatemala. There were also a large number of North Americans in Guatemala working on the construction of the large military airfield. . . . These many men gave added impetus to the need for a permanent English-speaking church."

The Union Church, Guatemala City, in 2003.

Men and their wives and families. My father had started going in April of 1956, and my mother and I joined him when we arrived in August of that year. In Phoenix, we had been members of the Trinity Episcopal Church located in the center of the city. At age four and five, I thought it was very big, an adobe-colored building glimmering in the desert sun. It shrank as I got older and now stands surrounded by other buildings.

There were midnight Christmas services lighted only by candles, and new dresses, shoes, and socks for Easter Sunday. And some of the teenage girls in our neighborhood organized a weekly summer Bible school, which centered on Bible stories told with a felt board, which would simply hold the cut-out figures of the various characters with no tape or staples. I was completely taken by this fact, focusing on it and not on the lesson at all.

Many of my parents' friends were members of the Union Church, and looking back, I see that it clearly served as a social club for these Americans trying to figure out how to live in a developing country. There was a Women's Auxiliary, which was responsible for providing coffee and cake after the service. The coffee was poured from large ornate silver pots into delicate porcelain cups.

There were bake sales, a thrift shop, and the Christmas pageant in which, one year, I was given the role of Mary. The Baby Jesus was represented by a light bulb nestled deep in a wicker basket. I repeatedly checked the basket, trying to grasp the significance of this.

I have the sense that the Union Church was a social gathering place for Americans living in Guatemala City because I don't remember my father having any particular enthusiasm for church-going or stories from his New Mexico childhood pertaining to church. I'm sure that, in Phoenix, he went because my mother wanted him to.

She had been raised Methodist in Illinois but recognized the apparent social benefits of being an Episcopalian, hence our attendance at Trinity Episcopal in Phoenix. And in Guatemala City, they both enjoyed and benefited from the weekly contact with other Americans. But I sensed that my father's enthusiasm for the actual proceedings of the service was limited. He had developed an uncanny instinct for the exact moment the sermon was about to start and, in the thirty seconds before, would leave the pew and go outside into the courtyard to smoke a cigarette. He would return right when the sermon ended and stay for the rest of the service. This visibly annoyed my mother, as her dear hope was that we would all attend the complete service together—and that he would stop smoking, but she never scolded him about it.

Ceil as the Virgin Mary, *c.* 1957.

I think that, in addition to not wanting to be preached at, after having worked a very long week, he deeply resented having to put on a suit and tie and tight dress shoes and behave respectably on a Sunday when he would have to get up and go to work less than twenty-four hours later. His idea of Sunday was to relax around the house, maybe go out for a meal, but no suit or tie.

I inherited my father's stance about church proceedings but showed it in different ways. There was my earlier misplaced focus on the felt board and the light bulb in the wicker basket. The Union Church, of course, offered Sunday school for the children of the congregation, and I was enrolled in it. My father had a very large collection of religious jokes with a wide range of appropriateness, and he routinely shared them with friends and acquaintances. I had picked up some of them, and Sunday school seemed like the perfect venue to share what I had learned, "So Jesus says to Saint Peter. . . ." I'm sure that I didn't understand many of jokes. The very distressed and confused Sunday school teacher contacted my mother—no doubt face to face, as we didn't own a phone. "Are you and your husband aware that Ceil is telling religious jokes during our Sunday school lessons?" While I didn't completely understand what the problem was, I stopped after a firm talking to. I'm sure that my father had a good laugh about it along with a deep sense of pride—"That's my girl!"—which he knew not to share.

A completely different exposure to church in Guatemala came with the Christmas and Easter processions carried out by the Catholic Guatemalans. At Christmas time, I was allowed to join our maid in wearing a long, dark-blue, woven skirt, a white cotton shirt with short, puffy sleeves, and best of all, many strands of multicolored glass beads that shattered very easily. The blue dye of the skirt was not color-fast and rubbed off onto my thighs and knees. A small amount of rouge was applied to my cheeks and lips. We would walk hand in hand in the processions to a nearby Catholic church with many people dressed in the same way, the men with multicolored woven pants, white shirts, and peasant hats. At one point, everyone genuflected and crossed themselves, and I, of course, did the same. This caused great concern to my Methodist/Episcopalian mother when it was reported to her. One such event was the festival of the Virgin of Guadalupe on December 12. The procession was followed by large bonfires at many homes around the city, their purpose being to chase away the evil spirits and usher in the Christmas season.

During Easter Week in the city of Antigua, the residents made bright colored carpets of sawdust on several of the main streets. Making these carpets required at least two days of work by hand on one's knees, and the images were then destroyed within a half-hour as processions marched over them. In these processions on Maundy Thursday, Good Friday, and Easter Sunday, the faithful carried enormous platforms each containing a relevant biblical scene: Roman soldiers tormenting Jesus, Mary and Mary Magdalene mourning his death, and the crucifixion itself with Jesus, the cross, and more Roman soldiers. All the figures were bigger than life-size. Each platform had a mahogany base and was carried by at least thirty men dressed in the white cotton pants and tunics worn by farmers. These platforms were kept in the church during the year and returned there after the procession.

As of this writing, these processions continue and have gained international attention; they are attended by thousands of visitors from all over the world. In the late 1950s, they were a local event, known to a much smaller audience.

The Union Church of Guatemala was also one site where American parents worked in a focused way to maintain aspects of American culture for their children whom, they assumed, would at some point return to the United States. Hence, my induction into the Brownies in the fellowship hall of the church. The children being inducted could not possibly share their parents' understanding of this event, most of us having been brought to live in Guatemala as five-year-olds or younger. As with many other things—Halloween, Thanksgiving—we had no insight into the American context of which the Brownies were a part, but we went along with the proceedings.

The uniform was worn on meeting days, with saddle shoes. There were various organized activities, and shortly before we moved to Rome, there was the "flying up" ceremony which marked the transition from Brownies to full-fledged Girl Scouts with their green uniforms. In the middle of the hall, some of the men in the congregation had constructed a bridge with a railing on each side, two steps on each end, and a very large mirror underneath to represent the water being crossed over. The bridge was beautifully decorated with garlands of flowers and was altogether enchanting. Some very solemn words were spoken for and by each girl being "flown up," and each of us then proceeded across the bridge. Membership in the Girl Scouts would continue in Rome.

Ceil in her Brownie uniform, 1958.

The fellowship hall at the Union Church included a stage, complete with curtains, wings, and steps at each end that brought the stage up to a level above the floor of the hall. Members of the congregation produced plays for the enjoyment of the community, and it was this stage that gave me, at age six, an instantaneous understanding of how theatre works. The play being produced was *The Man Who Came to Dinner,* a comedy in three acts by George S. Kaufman and Moss Hart. A play clearly meant for an adult audience. I had occasion to be in the fellowship hall one day, maybe after the church service. The curtains of the stage were open, and my attention was captured by the very realistic living room that had been set up. I climbed up the stairs and began to explore the set. A real sofa, real lamps, a real table. Plastic flowers. At the back of the set was a very real looking wall with pictures hung on it, just as I saw at home. And in the wall was a door with a handle on it. I approached the door and turned the handle, fully expecting to see other rooms of the house. But behind the door was the storage area for the theatre with cardboard boxes, chairs, and folded card tables. The illusion that theatre creates came to me in a thrilling flash, "Oh, a whole seemingly real environment can be created, and people can tell stories there, but it's not a real place; it's a pretend place, like the pretend places I make at home!"

As I had been taken to church in Phoenix and in Guatemala, I continued to be taken in Rome. I started to realize fairly early on that my attention wandered. What always got my attention in Phoenix and Guatemala were the light of the candles in a dark cathedral, the magic of felt boards, the vibrant colors of the costumes and the beads, the power and smell of the bonfires, the astonishing precision and short-lived beauty of the saw-dust carpets—in short, the intense visual spectacle that humans are driven to realize in the context of faith. I'm pretty sure that I was always meant to be focusing mainly on something else, but I did not. I was consistently—but not yet willfully—missing the main point.

Times have changed markedly. The February 1, 2015, bulletin from the Union Church states, "We believe that the Bible is the God breathed and plenarily inspired Word of God, infallible in its original manuscripts. The Bible (66 books of the Old and New Testament) is our supreme and final authority in faith and life." Period. Such a blunt declaration never appeared in the bulletin in the late 1950s, and it doesn't even appear in a 2003 version.

The Union Church, though certainly a church, had also clearly served as a fairly relaxed gathering place for Protestant expats of all denominations. Things have tightened up, maybe as a response to the widespread Protestant evangelism among Guatemalans, non-existent in the late 1950s; maybe a response to being Protestant in a predominantly Catholic country, or as an extension of the evangelism that has come to prominence in the United States and that these expatriates bring with them to Guatemala. All of the above, maybe. This is a different Union Church, for sure.

Esquipulas

My parents and I traveled a lot during our four years in Guatemala. We drove several times down to Puerto San José on the Pacific Coast with its striking black volcanic sand. It opened as a port in 1853 and was Guatemala's main shipping terminal for many years.

There is a point in the drive down from Guatemala City, not too far outside Escuintla, this Pacific region's largest town, where you can physically feel the drop into tropical Guatemala. The temperature suddenly rises, the humidity closes in, and the road seems to have dropped down to a lower level. Vendors appear along the road in wooden lean-tos, selling bananas, mangos, and pineapples.

Even in the late 1950s, the town of San José already showed its hundred-year age, with worn wooden buildings and rough streets. Its great pier extended out into the water. We were warned of strong rip currents. I see photos of it today, the wide beach covered with tourists down from the city, and it doesn't seem as fierce.

Another trip took us to the Castillo de San Felipe, where the Rio Dulce and Lake Isabal meet. Its construction started in 1595 as a response to the disruption of commercial trade by pirates. Despite the designation as *castillo*, it was really more of a fort. It later became a prison. I remember running around the ramparts and exploring the dark, cool passages inside, a relief from the close tropical air outside.

We traveled in 1958 to the Mayan ruins of Tikal near the town of Flores in the northern Petén jungle of Guatemala. We made the long journey in a borrowed jeep, with many sections near the ruins consisting of a dirt road or no road. At one point, we forded a jungle stream.

The site now spans about six square miles, with some four thousand structures, including a number of mighty temples. An introductory walking tour now requires three hours. In 1958, only part of Temple I, Temple of the Jaguar, had been excavated, along with the ball court next to it. The excavators quickly discovered that machine excavation damaged the distinctive steps of the temples and that the work on the numerous huge structures and the surrounding buildings would have to proceed by hand. Temples are still being discovered and worked on.

Puerto San José, Guatemala, in the 1950s.

We stayed inside the park in the Jaguar Inn. Our room was distinguished by a 40-watt bulb hanging from the ceiling. We ate in the hotel dining room and explored what little there was to see.

The drive from Guatemala City to the eastern town of Esquipulas, on the border with Honduras is a challenge in itself. It is 1958 and as soon as we leave the Pan American Highway, we are on dirt roads, the car kicking up high dust as we go. I am seven years old.

On the road to Esquipulas, Guatemala, 1958.

The faded photograph shows three Indian men carrying their terra cotta pots, three large bags of them, to market. We are in the eastern highlands of the country, near the borders of Honduras and El Salvador, and we're on our way to see the sixteenth-century Baroque cathedral famous for pilgrimages, the Basilica del Cristo Negro. On the altar stands a large dark balsam wood crucifix. Carved in 1594, the statue has a reputation for responding to prayers of all kinds and for performing miracles.

As we approach the main street of the town, we see what it is famous for: people descending the mile-long road to the cathedral on their knees, praying the rosary as they go.

Castillo de San Felipe ramparts, Guatemala, 1958.

Castillo de San Felipe, Guatemala, 1958.

They are of course in serious pain, their knees screaming for attention, but their devotion is obviously very deep.

"Why are they crying, Mommy?" I ask, and she tries to explain. "They're going to see the statue of Jesus in the church," she says.

This was new to me. I couldn't remember anyone at Trinity Episcopal in Phoenix or the Union Church in Guatemala City moving towards the altar on his or her knees while crying. The plaza in front of the church had a carnival air, with stands selling food and drinks and souvenirs for the pilgrims.

Basilica del Cristo Negro, Esquipulas, Guatemala, 1958.

The road to Basilica del Cristo Negro, Esquipulas, Guatemala, 1958.

This trip could have been a cruel anthropological exploration of various forms of devotion, but it ended up unexpectedly contributing one of the more hilarious episodes to my childhood memories.

In 1958, there's no Holiday Inn with an outside pool in Esquipulas, Guatemala, and no way to call ahead to reserve a room. My parents obviously have the name of a boarding house in the town. We end up there, sharing a room with another family of three, with only a sheet hung on a rope across the room as a divider. The bathroom is in the hall, and there is of course no television. After dinner, when it is dark, we simply go to bed. We think that we are settling down for a restful sleep when suddenly the silence is shattered by a roar of flatulence coming from the other side of the sheet. In case we are wondering if we have imagined it, it is followed by another roar.

At this point, my father bursts out laughing, and we also hear the wife of the offender strongly admonishing him in Spanish. We are now all laughing audibly and collapse helplessly when we hear the offender say, in protest, *"Es solo mi boca."* ("It's only my mouth") in an attempt to convince everyone that he is merely imitating flatulence with his mouth.

Everyone on both sides of the sheet is now howling in the dark. We all finally fall asleep, and by the time we leave the room in the morning, our roommates are long gone. We never see them face to face.

The phrase, "*es solo mi boca*," of course, entered our family repertoire and found uses in many situations.

Our last trip in Guatemala took place when we left in the very early summer of 1960. I was so stunned to be told that we would be leaving I cried on and off for three days. "We seriously wondered if we had made a mistake in deciding to move to Italy," my mother later said. I was homesick for Guatemala before we even left, a sharp knot in my throat. But leave we did.

The plan was to drive north through Mexico to Phoenix. At one point, the Mexican highway was still under construction, so our car was loaded onto a flat train car with no walls, and we rode through central Mexico peering out the car windows at the scraggly and mostly uninhabited landscape. We ate out of cans for those few days and toileted using an old coffee can. We were eventually back on the road and driving into Nogales, Arizona, on our way up to Phoenix.

Reading in a moving car makes me vaguely carsick, so during all these travels through Guatemala, I amused myself in the back seat by singing or making up word games or quite simply looking out the window. And that was enough. There were no video machines in cars in those days or the tablets that I now see advertised on television. There was no anxiety expressed about a need to keep children's minds occupied at all moments while they traveled. Looking out the window was considered quite enough, and it was. The passing sights on all these trips fed my mind. As an adult, I always have newspapers, books, or magazines with me for trips on buses or trains, but they usually remain unopened. I'm looking out the window.

BERT'S SIDE

SO WHAT OF THESE PARENTS OF MINE? What family history shaped them before they shaped me? How were they shaped so they could make the decision to move, both of them at age forty-six, from the United States, first to Guatemala and then to Italy? I want to pause momentarily to take a look at the direct line that runs between the narrative of those who came before me and my own.

My father was William Albertrand Lucas, known to all as Bert.

Longbridge Deverill is one of six Deverill villages in the County of Wiltshire in the south-central part of England, "where the western edge of Salisbury Plain dips into Somerset. Longbridge is the main village and its parish includes neighbouring Crockerton. The other Deverills are Hill, now in Longbridge parish, Brixton, Monkton, and Kingston."

The history of Wiltshire tells us that the Deverill Valley, named for the River Deverill, has been continuously inhabited since at least 3500 BC and that until World War II, the main source of employment was farming. This is where Robert Lucas was born in 1630 and lived until he was forty-nine. He and his family were Quakers. Actually, they became Quakers; Robert's family goes back at least four generations, with the earliest attested being Daniel A. de Lucas, born in Kent in 1500.

The results of my DNA test say "6% Iberian Peninsula," so this may explain the "de." Almost impossible to nail this down. Daniel's son James, born in 1526 also in Kent, was knighted in 1571; this evidently was the occasion for the dropping of the "de."

Not satisfied with the Church of England, George Fox founded the Society of Friends in 1651. The first meeting was held in Durham in 1653. Fox and those like him did not see a need for a formal clergy or for paying tithes to the church; they felt that God could speak directly to anyone through Jesus. As is known, they came to be known as "Quakers" because they were said to quake in the presence of God. One of the most well-known of them, William Penn, invited his fellow Friends to join him in a "Holy Experiment" in America. King Charles II had granted him ownership of what is now known as Pennsylvania in 1681, and Penn arrived there in 1682. The Quaker Act of 1662 had made it illegal to refuse to take the Oath of Allegiance to the Crown; the subsequent Conventicle Act of 1664 made a criminal of anyone who did not pledge allegiance to the Crown or who held secret meetings. The Quakers believed that it was wrong to take "superstitious" oaths and continued to hold secret meetings. Twenty years after these acts and the imprisonment of many Quakers, William Penn left for America. King James II issued a general pardon in 1686 and over twelve hundred Quakers were released from prison.

Robert Lucas was part of a community of Quakers in County Wiltshire. However, the Quaker community in Wiltshire gradually declined until 1750, and then very rapidly after that and strikingly, there was a shift from Quakerism to Methodism. He saw fit to leave in 1679, three years before William Penn. He had already lived forty-nine of his fifty-eight years in Longbridge Deverill. He clearly made the decision that a huge step into the unknown was a better choice than staying in England. In *Emigrants to Pennsylvania, 1641–1819*, Michael Tepper describes how Robert's huge step took him to the ship *Elizabeth and Mary*, upon whose passenger list his name appears: "Robert Lucas, of Deverall, Longbridge, in the County of Wilts, yeoman. Arrived in this river [in Philadelphia] the 4th of the 4th Month, in the 'Elizabeth and Mary,' of Waymouth."

Elizabeth, his wife "arrived on the ship 'Conent,' of London."

By 1681, Robert and a William Biles had been appointed as justices of the peace in Bucks County. Robert and Elizabeth were present at the first Burlington Monthly Meeting in 1681, in Burlington, New Jersey. By 1683, Robert was a member of the provincial assembly. He was a member of the first Assembly under William Penn in 1682 and 1683, and signed the Great Seal of Rights in Philadelphia in 1683. By then, he and Elizabeth were attending the Falls Monthly Meeting in Bucks County, Pennsylvania.

A 1687 map entitled "A map of the improved part of Province of Pennsilvania in America: begun by Wil. Penn, Proprietary and Governour thereof anno 1681" shows the first tract of land they owned in 1679, 177 acres fronting on the Delaware River, confirmed by William Penn in 1684.

As cited in *Documents Relating to the Colonial History of the State of New Jersey, Volume I. 1631–1687,* Robert and his son John had petitioned Governor Carteret of New Jersey for this land as soon as they arrived in 1679:

Honerble Sir

Wee whose names ar here vnder subscribed lately come ffrom old England with Intent to inhabit in this country And if yor Hono^r please to Grant vs and order vnder yor hand too setle . . . ; wee may have land in Jersie side but we ar willing to become Tennants to his Highness the Duke of yourke, if yor Hono^r pleas to giue vs the grant and to cleer the Indians. . . .

Your Humble Servants although vnknoun Robert Lucas John Lucas . . .

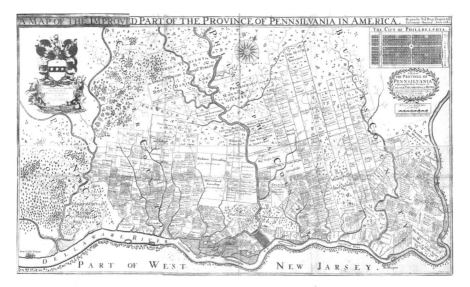

Map of Pennsylvania, 1687 (Library of Congress, Geography and Map Division)

These "Indians" would have been the Lenni Lenape, "original people" in their language.

In *A Genealogical and Personal History of Bucks County*, William Davis states:

> Before the arrival of Europeans, Bucks county was occupied, and the soil owned by Indians known as the Lenni Lenape, who dwelt on both banks of the Delaware from its mouth to its source, and reaching to the Susquehanna in the interior. They were divided into a number of minor tribes, speaking as many dialects of the same common language. The English called them the Delaware Indians because they lived upon that river. The greater portion of those who lived within the present limits of the county were known as Neshaminies, probably from the name of one of our largest and most beautiful streams. The Lenni Lenapes originally came from the valley of the Mississippi, whence they were driven by more powerful neighbors, and sought a quiet home on the banks of the Delaware. Europeans found them a mild, amiable and kindly-disposed people; and, on their first arrival, the Indians assisted to feed them, and in some instances, the early settlers would probably have starved without the friendly help of their red neighbors. . . . Isaac Still was a celebrated Indian, of good education, and the leader of the last remnant of the Delaware tribe adjacent to Philadelphia. His only son, Joshua, was educated at Germantown. In 1771 Isaac Still moved up into Buckingham where he collected the scattered remains of his tribe, and in 1775, he, with 40 persons, started off to the Wabash. . . . Among the prominent Indians, natives of the county, were Captain Harrison, born in Buckingham and intended for the Delaware chieftain, and Teedyuscung, a man of superior natural abilities, who spoke English and could read and write.

Davis also states, "Before Penn left England, many persons had purchased land in Pennsylvania to whom deeds were given, the surveys to be made after their arrival."

Pretty damn amazing that this land, called Lattiniconk by its Indian inhabitants and very clearly occupied for hundreds of years before the arrival of William Penn and Robert Lucas, could be sold from over thirty-five hundred miles away, sight unseen. Sold and then occupied with its original occupants sent packing—"cleered [of] the Indians," as Robert Lucas requested in his petition. My Robert Lucas, my first ancestor in America.

Detail of 1687 map. Robert Lucas's land indicated by the arrow
(Library of Congress, Geography and Map Division).

Isaac Lucas, Civil War Record.

A second tract of land, 322 acres, was west of the Delaware and was sold to Lucas by William Penn.

Robert Lucas lived in Bucks County until his death in 1688. He had come to America a full ninety-seven years before the Revolution; he had come to the Colonies. In an ironic twist, Robert's grandson Edward, born in Bucks County in 1710, married a non-Quaker, Mary

Darke. For this, in 1736, he was disowned by the Society of Friends for marrying "out of unity." Census records and various accounts show him ending up in what is now Shepherdstown, West Virginia—the colony of Virginia at that time. He was eventually reinstated in the Society of Friends and died in 1777 in Martinsburg, Berkeley County, Virginia, by then referred to as part of the United Colonies. Ironic that the same people who had left England to escape the oppression of their religion were quite ready to expel one of their own for "marrying out."

Edward's son Robert was born in 1740 in Frederick County, Virginia, and the record states that he was wounded in Western Virginia and killed by Indians in Nashville, Tennessee, in 1781.

By 1816, my branch of the family was in Ohio, where Newton Lucas was born in Hamilton County on December 29 of that year. His father, Benjamine, had been a member of the Antioch Christian Church in Clinton County, Indiana, so evidently the Lucases were no longer Quakers. By the time Newton's son Isaac was born in 1846, the family was in Frankfort, Indiana. Isaac's Civil War pension request showed that he enrolled in Company K, 154th Regiment of the Indiana Infantry and served from April 4 to August 4 of 1865, barely four months. He was nineteen years old.

By 1872, Isaac is in Kansas, where my grandfather Alfred Edgar, known as Allie Edgar or A. E. to all, was born. The *Morning Reporter* (Independence, Kansas) on April 18, 1889, announces the first Oklahoma Land Rush to be held April 22 and shouts, "They are all in!" The sub-headlines go on to state that "Sturdy Homeseekers and Scheming Speculators Cross the Line at the Appointed Hour," and the article describes a city of tents and shanties in Guthrie, Oklahoma.

The April 24 edition describes the first two women to stake claims, Mrs. R. R. Hersting and Mrs. Anna Beard, widows from Arkansas City.

The Indians witnessing the rush are called the "betwixt and be-tweens," and "the squaw men, their squaws and pappooses [*sic*], looked on in open mouthed wonder at train after train load [*sic*] of honest white people who went through what would soon be another section of the coming great territory of Oklahoma."

THEY ARE ALL IN!

THE LAND NO LONGER PROMISED.

Sturdy Homeseekers and Scheming Speculators Cross the Line at the Appointed Hour.

A City of Tents and Shanties at Guthrie, Where all Was Open Country in the Morning.

Thousands of People Happy Possessors of Town Lots on That City's Site.

IN AT LAST.

GUTHRIE, Oklahoma, April 22.—Lieutenant Foster, of Company G, Fifth cavalry, stood at the north line of Oklahoma, watch in hand. Guards held a rope marking the line. When the noon hour came he turned to the bugler and told him to give the signal. The bugler blew the blast and immediately there sprang across the line with a loud yell and cheering, a thousand riders, urging their horses on at the fullest speed. Behind they left their wagons, family and supplies, expecting them to follow. Many a man had paid $500 for a horse for this special occasion, for much depended upon the result of the race. Others rode a horse and took a second as a relay.

It was a race for valuable lands and everyone went at the full trot of his speed. On, on they flew, first in a bunch, then separating they spread in all directions. Many kept in a bee line for Guthrie, others went to the southeast, while a few rode to the southwest. In ten minutes some of the fleetest were three miles to the south and were still going on at full speed

lots commenced in the morning illegally was now continued under the law. Two women, the first to take claims in Oklahoma, Mrs. R. R. Hesting and Mrs. Anna Beard, two widows of Arkansas City, went upon the hillside near the land office and sat down upon their lots. People commenced to stretch ropes. Soon in the distance a man came riding in at full speed upon a fine horse. He said he had come from thirty-five miles east. If he did he had made the distance in fifteen minutes if he had started at 12 o'clock.

It was 1:20 o'clock when the first train of ten cars came rolling in from the north. It was densely packed and crowded, and the people commenced to roll to the platform from the domes of the baggage cars and off the tops of the cars. Baggage, tents and supplies were pitched from the windows. Before the train had stopped many of the passengers had alighted from the cars. They commenced running up the hill to the land office and passed all the lots staked out before and then continued until they found a place which had no claimant. Every man had in his hand a hatchet, or an ax and carried four pegs with which to mark the boundaries of his lots. With each succeeding train there came in new town lot seekers. The last train from the north was as heavily loaded as the first and the scramble and the excitement at the unloading as intense.

Upon the hillside east of the station stood the only frame building. It was 16x20, one story, unpainted. Near the railroad track had been put up the first hotel in Oklahoma. It was opened by General J. N. Reece. Colonel Jake Wheeler and Colonel J. C. Bell, of Springfield, Ill., and called the Santa Fe house. The hotel consists of fifty tents, five large ones being used as dining rooms, with a capacity of 200 beds. The register for the first day showed thirty-seven names, and for the first day over 500.

The postoffice was on top of the hill, south of the land office. It was a wall tent, with a sign "Postoffice" above the entrance. Just north was another tent, above which waved a flag. It was the headquarters of the United States marshal.

AMONG THE FIRST.

The first man to get the attention of the land office authorities was M. B. Cahn, of Arkansas City, who filed, as attorney, ten homesteads for old soldiers.

The name appearing first upon the books is Thomas Johnson, his claim being the northwest quarter of section 8, township 10 south, range 2 west.

The first papers of arrest were issued by Marshal Needles for the arrest of a pick-

hotels, streets, and everything in general has once more come back to their normal condition. With the exception of the large wagon trains of freight, few wagons are to be seen moving south on the trail.

FILINGS.

One boomer, sitting on the depot platform at Arkansas City this morning, expressed his and the sentiments of a good many others, if they would be honest enough to tell them, when he said: "If any fellow comes along and wants my claim he'll have to lick me, and if he does, I'll be like the boy was when the calf kicked him. I wont say a d— word."

The boomers evacuated Arkansas City in eight trains of nine cars each train carrying about one thousand people. The floors of the waiting rooms in the Arkansas City depot last night were covered with boomers packed in like sardines. Conspicuous in the crowds of boomers were veterans in their G. A. R. uniforms. Some of them could not restrain their patriotism, but went about carrying, wearing or waving the American flag. The favorite emblem of the tiller on a claim was a flag.

As the trains would rush past where a settler had located, that worthy would wave triumphantly if as to say "go in and get what you can. I've got what I want." The "monarch of all he surveys" was fellow who "got thar and squatted" on the choice piece of ground.

Those "betwixt and betweens," the squaw men, their squaws and pappooses, looked on in open mouthed wonder at the train after train load of honest white people who went through what will soon be another section of the coming great territory of Oklahoma.

The young chap who swung himself under the car and rode on the trucks of car, was promptly named "Oklahoma Eli." He got thar and got a lot.

A prominent young Wichita attorney, who was going down on the train to Arkansas City, Sunday night, earned the name of the Great Oklahoma Gallant. At Mulvane he assisted a very pretty and very refined young lady on the train and tried to obtain for her a seat in the car where the Wichita boys were. She was about to be seated when she happened to catch a glimpse of ——, he is one of the Eagle Rifles—and said: "No I thank you. I prefer the smoking car," and the young attorney there procured for her a seat, in a double seat with three boomers of the boomest kind, one of whom monopolized her conversation, while Mr. —— could only stand by and listen. When she got off the train at Winfield, she thanked her escort and gave him a lilac spray which he planted on his corner lot down here in Guthrie.

Morning Reporter, Independence, Kansas, April 18, 1889 (Kansas Historical Society).

By 1889, Isaac and A. E. were living in Elk City, Kansas, very near the Oklahoma border, and made plans to join the 1889 Land Rush. Isaac was forty-three, and A. E. was seventeen. The Territory of Oklahoma was an organized, incorporated territory of the United States that had existed since May 2, 1890. And, as in Pennsylvania and Delaware in 1679, it was not as though this land was unoccupied. Quite the contrary: for centuries before the Indian Intercourse Act of 1834, Indians had used the land exclusively.

The Indian Intercourse Act (also known as the Indian Nonintercourse Act) is the collective name given to six statutes passed by the Congress in 1790, 1793, 1796, 1799, 1802, and 1834. The act regulates commerce between Americans and Native Americans. The most notable provisions of the act regulate the inalienability of aboriginal title in the United

States, a continuing source of litigation for almost two hundred years. The prohibition on purchases of Indian lands without the approval of the federal government has its origins in the Royal Proclamation of 1763 and the Confederation Congress Proclamation of 1783.

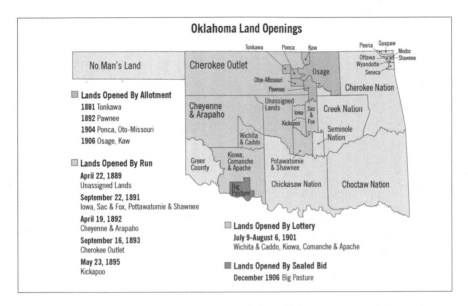

Oklahoma land openings. (Courtesy of the Oklahoma Historical Society.)

A quick glance at a map of the Oklahoma Territory at the time of the first land rush shows at least twenty-eight Indian tribes, at least eight of which were in the so-called Unassigned Lands, a term popularized in 1879.

The 1889 rush was to the Cherokee Strip, according to Robert Lucas in the *Quarterly of the Oklahoma Historical Society*, "a narrow piece of land about two and one-fourth miles north of the 37th parallel in southern Kansas, extending west from the Cherokee Neutral Lands to the 100th meridian. . . . This strip of land, a result of a boundary dispute with Kansas, was ceded to the United States [along with other land], by the Cherokees in 1866."

Isaac's son Robert tells his niece Lucille that "Isaac Lucas, everyone called him Ike, was a big man, five or six inches over six feet, with blue eyes that looked right through you. By the time I remember him, his thick, dark hair and the handlebar mustache was graying. Eventually, both turned snow white. Everyone who knew him said that his word 'was as good as gold.' I might add that when my father made up his mind to do something, he did it, and he made up his mind to establish a homestead in the Oklahoma Territory."

The land rush started on April 22, but the homestead was not to be. After staking a claim west of present-day Oklahoma City, Isaac contracted typhoid fever and was forced to return to Kansas. The newspapers started carrying stories about another land opening in the Oklahoma Territory. "The Towns All 'Soonered' by Hired Men," stated the *Elk City Enterprise* (Kansas) on September 25, 1893. This would be the 1893 land rush known as the Cherokee Strip, and Isaac did participate in this one. It opened on Saturday, September 16, 1893, as documented in the photo, "The start of the run at 12:00 noon, 10 seconds after the start."

The start of the Land Run of 1893 (Thomas N. Athey Collection, courtesy of the Oklahoma Historical Society, #5003).

Isaac tells Lucille that Isaac and A. E. both experienced difficulty getting up the bank of the Cimarron River with their horses and wagons but once they made it, they followed:

> the old Indian trail for about twelve or thirteen miles. My father staked his claim in Pawnee County, ten miles south and ten miles east of Pawnee. Jennings soon became the nearest trading place, four miles east of his homestead. Al [A. E.] flagged his claim and staked it next to my father's and later, to keep anybody from jumping

their claims, they cut logs from the trees and laid them in a square to indicate where they would build their cabins. . . . There was an abundance of trees on my father's homestead—oak, burr oak, post oak—from which he acquired the necessary lumber to construct fences and buildings that he lived in the first winter. . . . After my father constructed his log cabin, in late February or early spring, he returned to Kansas for the rest of the family. . . . We had three wagons of farm equipment, household goods and supplies; five teams of horses, a span of mules, and some other stock, including saddle-horses. We also brought Peking ducks, chickens and almost anything else that anyone would need to start a farm.

In fact, the September 15 edition of the *Elk City Enterprise* (Kansas) describes the Santa Fe freight trains as "heavy with emigrant cars of household goods, horses, cattle and implements." The August 25 edition lists the conditions set by President Benjamin Harrison governing settlers taking up lands, including: "No railroad trains will be allowed to run through the strip on the day of the opening so that parties who may intend to charter a train in order to get an advantage that way will be prevented."

Isaac B. Lucas grave.

Odd Fellows Cemetery, Maramec, Oklahoma.

From a twenty-first-century American perspective, the notion that any shelter had to be built from the ground up, trees had to be logged before houses could be built, and fields cleared before anything could be planted is striking. This not only for Isaac and A. E. in what would become the state of Oklahoma in 1907 but also for Robert Lucas and his family in Pennsylvania: intense and exhausting physical labor to get through before a life could be imagined, all without electrical power, running water, or mechanized farm equipment.

Probably more striking is the fact that, until not that long before Isaac and A. E. staked their claims, the Pawnee Indians had occupied the very same land and had led their lives there. As with the Lenni Lenape in Pennsylvania, the Pawnee were simply told that they would have to go. Leave their homes and go.

Isaac stayed in Oklahoma for the rest of his life; he died in 1940 in Gideon at age ninety-four and is buried in the Odd Fellows Cemetery, in Maramec, Oklahoma. Given that his life spanned the years between 1846 and 1940, I imagined interviewing him and saying, "You were born in Indiana in 1846 and raised there and then came to Kansas after the Civil War, in which you fought very briefly. And you died in Oklahoma in December of 1940, at age ninety-four. By then, you had seen World War I and missed seeing another one by just a year. By 1940, there were telephones and refrigerators and cars and planes. Your daughter says that, during the Rush, you cut logs from trees and built your cabins from the ground up. You had to bring with you anything that you needed; you couldn't just go to a store and buy it. Everything was from scratch and by hand. What I have always wanted to ask is simply this: what was it like to live in those years between 1846 and 1940? The changes that you witnessed in the world and in your life seem almost too much to absorb." I have imagined his response: "The simple answer is that the changes that took place over my lifetime simply boggled the mind. As we cleared land and built cabins by hand in Oklahoma and as we hid behind trees to avoid Confederate fire at the end of the war, it never entered our minds that one day we would watch airplanes fly overhead or ride in them, drive into town in our cars, and store food in an icebox that plugged into the wall. We would have told you that you were crazy to suggest any of that. The changes took place fairly slowly over time, yes, but to stand and look back to life as it was in 1846 is almost confusing, as if we had been on another planet.

"Mine were a very particular ninety-four years to be alive because of the changes that took place. More probably happened in those ninety-four years than in any other ninety-four-year stretch in history. For a white person, each change was basically for the better—except I do wonder about WW I. This of course can't be said for black folks or for Indians, whom we basically pushed out of the way in 1893. They had been there hundreds of years and were now told to leave, period. And except for the promise of 1865 and some elections to Congress, these ninety-four years for black folks just continued what had come before and, in some ways, were worse because the promise of freedom could be seen but not grasped.

"So, dear Ceil, the answer is that it depends on where you were sitting. I had a pretty good seat."

A. E. Lucas and Cornelia Jane Eidson, 1908, wedding photo.

A. E. moved on to the Territory of New Mexico by way of Texas. He married my grandmother Cornelia Jane Eidson in 1908 in Dalhart, and by 1910, they were in Vaughn, New Mexico.

The 1910 census shows A. E., Cornelia Jane, my father at age four months—he was born in December of 1909, and the census was taken in April—and my father's half-sister Ruby, A. E.'s daughter from an earlier marriage. A photo taken slightly after the census shows the family in front of their house. My father is clearly old enough to walk, almost two, so this is probably mid-1911. He is blond and has a bowl haircut. To his left is A. E., and next to A. E., his mother Cornelia Jane. The other two people in the photo live in the other side of the duplex. Both of the men have donned their requisite hats, and both of the women have impossibly small waists, pinched in no doubt by corsets.

Two neighbors and Bert (*center*), A. E. *(left of Bert)*, a
nd Cornelia Jane *(left of A. E.)* Lucas in Vaughn, New Mexico.

The house is very trim and tidy, stark on the central New Mexico plain. A later photo, following, shows the family in a posed photo when my father is about ten.

A. E., Bert, and Jane Lucas, *c.* 1919.

Family lore had it that A. E. was a saloon keeper in Duran, located fourteen miles southwest of Vaughn, at the intersection of US Route 54 and New Mexico State Road 3 in Torrance County. The current population is about thirty-five. Duran was once a railroad division point. At the intersection stand the brick merchandise company with its high front and the whitewashed general merchandise store.

The merchandise company is the saloon that my grandfather ran. I visited it in 2005 and encountered an elderly gentleman living across from it. I told him that my grandfather had run the saloon and asked him who had owned it.

He said, "Those were the Courys."

I said, "Oh, C-u-r-r-y?" but as soon as I said it, I knew which Courys. Another spelling for the name is Khoury, Lebanese. And then I asked, "Who is Hindì?"

The gentleman said, "Oh, that's my father and uncle," who were also Lebanese.

At first, they sold pots and pans out of horse-drawn wagons; the Spanish-speaking residents of the area called them Los Arabes. Most of them were Muslims, but many set Islam aside and attended the St. John the Baptist Church in Duran. Since the mass was conducted in Spanish, most of them became trilingual.

Coury Merchandise Company, established 1908.

Coury Merchandise Company (courtesy of Land and Water USA).

Milhim (Bill) Hindì reached Las Vegas, New Mexico, in 1908 from Zahle in the Lebanese plains, and his brother Alex joined him in 1912. Alex married a woman named Clarita Duran, and the brothers decided to name the town after her. They opened the merchandise mart, and in 1920, they also started raising sheep. A sign on the Hindì store cheerily states, "Tourists welcome!" The elderly gentleman I met was Sam Coury, Alex's son. Striking that there was a Lebanese community in the dead center of New Mexico even before it became a state in 1912.

Hindì General Merchandise Store, established *c.* 1912.

1910 United States Federal Census for Lucas   SAVE ⌄

New Mexico › Guadalupe › Vaughn › District 0103   Related Content   Tools ⌄   Print

The Lucas family in the 1910 Federal Census
with A. E. as a saloonkeeper (National Archives).

As for what my family referred to as "the saloon," it was built around 1908 by Anton J. Coury as a general store and hotel. At one time, the lettering on the front promised: "sheep, wool, pelts." A player piano was delivered from a piano company in Colorado. On September 3, 1921, Anton J. Coury's business was robbed, and he was shot and killed. The business was continued on the same site until the late 1950s.

Finding actual evidence in the census of my grandfather as the saloon keeper of the Coury's business was one of a number of "holy shit!" moments that I have had in exploring my family history. My mother had mentioned it in passing, and I had tucked it away in my thoughts, but when it came up in very elegant handwriting in the column where occupations were listed, well, "Holy shit!" Spoken out loud, in the National Archives in Washington, DC. Some of the other patrons peered at me while others smiled knowing smiles.

A. E. died in 1931 at the age of fifty-nine. He is buried in Prescott, Arizona. He came a long way to Arizona, from Kansas through Oklahoma and New Mexico.

And we come directly to my father, William Albertrand Lucas, known to all as "Bert." He completed high school in Vaughn and had been accepted to the University of California, Berkeley. A. E. died in 1930, and Cornelia Jane married the ailing Clare Bradley. She had become a nurse, and the very frank arrangement was that she would take care of him in exchange for his supporting my father's college education. The story goes that Bert was accepted to the University of California, Berkeley and dutifully traveled there to start his freshman year in 1927. When he entered a lecture hall that had two hundred other freshmen, he left almost immediately and returned to the University of New Mexico in Albuquerque and reasonably sized classes. He was the first in his family to go to college and had never been out of New Mexico until his trip to California.

The photo below shows Bert on graduation day, age twenty-two. On his right is Bill Robson, an African American man who became his close friend during their college years. Bert graduated with a bachelor's degree in civil engineering, very good preparation for where he was headed: Guatemala, Rome, and the last stop, the World Bank in Washington, DC.

First stop, though, was civil engineering work in Northern Arizona—in the Navajo Nation—where he met Kathleen Kinnaman.

Bert Lucas (*right*) with Bill Robson (*center*).

KATHLEEN'S SIDE

My mother was Kathleen Kinnaman, known to her parents and brothers as Kack. My father called her Butchie, and many of her friends called her Patsy. The story of her family is somewhat more straightforward than Bert's.

Dunbar, Scotland, is located in East Lothian, on the southeast coast, about twenty-eight miles east of Edinburgh and twenty-eight miles from the English border. It was the site of the Battle of Dunbar in 1650. Oliver Cromwell was the leader of those in England against the idea of a monarchy, the monarch in question being Charles I. Charles I was executed in 1649, and a republic was declared, the Commonwealth of England, during which Scotland was ruled from England. The Scots had proclaimed Charles's son their king, Charles II. However, those in power in Scotland did not like the idea of engaging with King Charles II. They were mainly members of the militant Covenanter Kirk Party, strongly Presbyterian. Nevertheless, the King arrived in Scotland and was proclaimed King of Scots. This infuriated the English authorities. The English Parliamentarian forces under Oliver Cromwell invaded Scotland and defeated a Scottish army led by David Leslie, who was loyal to King Charles II. This was the Battle of Dunbar during which Cromwell killed four thousand Scots and imprisoned one thousand more. In *Scotland—The Story of a Nation*, Magnus Magnusson states, "The Scottish prisoners were marched south to slavery in the salt-mines in England or in the new plantations overseas. Hundreds died of disease and starvation on the way." Cromwell was subsequently named the Lord Protector of the Commonwealth and stayed in this role between 1653 and 1658.

It bears mentioning that things did not end that well for Cromwell. He died in 1658, of natural causes, and following his burial, he was dug up and "executed" again and decapitated. For a time, his head was displayed on a pole. In 1660, the monarchy was restored under Charles II.

Among the prisoners transported to the new plantations overseas following the Battle of Dunbar was John Kinninmont, Kathleen Kinnaman's first ancestor in America. (Included in the various spellings of the surname is the one he made when he came to Maryland—"Kinninmont" in Scotland became "Kininmont" in the Colonies.) He is on the list of prisoners: "Johne Kininmond, Ensign." There is a four-year period between the Battle of Dunbar and Kinninmont's transportation (1650–1654) during which he was probably held as an indentured servant, possibly involved in the draining of the Fens in East Anglia. The American colonies at that time included the Maryland Colony, and in 1654 he was transported to what is now known as Talbot County on Maryland's Eastern Shore, with the town of Easton as the county seat.

He had been born in 1634 in Dunfermline, a town in the southern part of Fife, just across the Firth of Forth from Edinburgh. The baptismal record shows November 26 as the day of his baptism. His father was Patrick; his mother was Mary Boswell, a descendant of King Robert the Bruce. Around 1200 AD, the "Kininmunds" were granted lands by the prior of St. Andrews. The name is Gaelic, "Cinn Fhinnmhonaidh," meaning "the head of the white hill." It's a safe bet that the Kininmunds of the thirteenth century were speakers of Scots Gaelic, but the anglicization of the Lowlands had begun in 1200 and was pretty much complete by 1600, so John Kinninmont would have been a native speaker of Scots English.

For transporting himself, his wife, and his children, John received two hundred acres from Cecilius Calvert, the second Lord Baltimore, plus an additional fifty acres for each child under the age of sixteen. Kininmont eventually owned roughly one thousand acres, which became known as the "Kininmont Plantation," in what is now Talbot County.

As the map shows, the property stood to the north of the Saint Michael's River, what is now known as the Miles River. The principal crop was tobacco and Kinninmont also planted corn. Most striking in considering Kinninmont's life is the amount of sheer physical labor required to make a living. The area still has towering stands of pine, hickory, and red and white oak, and we can see the areas that had to be cleared for planting to take place, cleared with no mechanized farm equipment at all.

As Matthew Kinnamont explains in *The Kinnamonts of the Eastern Shore of Maryland and the District of Columbia*, the method used by planters of tobacco and corn is known as "hoe culture." He adds:

> Unlike the plow and furrow agriculture of England, in which man and beast worked in concert to till the earth, the farming of Chesapeake tobacco and corn required at minimum a single hand and a single tool.
>
> Both indigenous crops were grown on individual hills of earth scraped together in the late spring by workers yielding broad hoes. Tobacco hills were usually spaced about four feet apart; corn hills, about six feet apart. Thus, one acre could accommodate 2,700 tobacco hills, or 1,210 corn hills.

MILES RIVER NECK, 1663-1688
ST. MICHAEL'S PARISH, TALBOT COUNTY, MARYLAND
Showing Locations of John Kininmont's Plantation, Dundee, Fentry, & Long Point

Kininmont Plantation (used with permission of Matthew Kinnamont).

But those planting hills were not available at all until the back-breaking work of clearing the huge trees was done. The task was helped with the Native American technique known as "girdling," whereby a deep band was cut into the tree, causing it to drop its leaves and branches and eventually die.

John Kinninmont lived the rest of his life in Maryland and passed in 1688 at age fifty-eight. He had come to the colony at age twenty-four and had made a full life there for thirty-four years.

It is one of the cardinal rules of doing genealogy that you will discover things you might not want to know. To wit, Maryland was a slave state: Maryland was founded in 1632, and as early as 1642, African slaves were brought to St. Mary's County to work on tobacco plantations. As we know, John Kininmont arrived from Scotland in 1654, and there were slaves, no doubt, on the Kininmont Plantation in Talbot County. The first federal census was done in 1790. In it, John's great-grandson John Thomas appears with one slave, still in Talbot County. By 1800, John and his wife, Eleanor, are in Stokes County, North Carolina, with two slaves listed. They are also shown in the 1810, 1820, and 1830 censuses with between two and four slaves, all female. John Thomas died in 1831. His son Philip made his way to Tennessee and was in Indiana by 1820, at age twenty. Philip's son Zachariah was born in Tennessee in 1816 but was also in Indiana with his family by 1820. His son Pleasant Columbus was born in Indiana, and the 1910 census lists him as the owner of a butcher shop. So, from 1654 through the 1830 census, 176 years of Kinnaman slaveholders. A very difficult part of being "from here" to come to terms with.

After five generations of farming, the family, now spelling their name Kinnaman, moved off the land for their livelihood. Pleasant's son Burren Oscar, my grandfather, settled in Decatur, Illinois, and worked as the mail clerk for the railroad.

My mother, Kathleen Kinnaman, was born on November 16, 1909 in Decatur with brothers Richard and Berkeley coming after her. Decatur was then, and is still, a very rural area, with Caterpillar Tractor and Archer Daniels Midland plants located there. But Burren Oscar was not a farmer. As an employee of the railroad, he was able to provide his daughter and sons a middle-class upbringing, even during the Depression.

In the photo on the next page, we see Kathleen on what is probably her first day at school in 1915 or 1916. She is six or seven, standing in front of a painted backdrop, so this is a posed photograph. She's ready for outdoor weather and looks so very bright and alert, as though she can barely contain her excitement. Kathleen carried in her DNA, completely, the wanderlust or, at least, the willingness to travel that brought the Kinnamans from Dunfermline, Scotland, to the Eastern Shore of Maryland in 1654.

Kathleen Kinnaman, age six or seven.

Kathleen was the first in her family to go to college and graduated in 1931 from Millikin University in Decatur with a degree in home economics. It was two years into the Depression, and there were no jobs to be had. There was something about further training in Chicago, but it wasn't long before she found herself a job as a dietician in a hospital in San Juan, Puerto Rico, 2,037 miles away from Decatur, as the crow flies, in a tropical climate. No discernible seasons. She might as well have been going to be a dietician on Saturn.

Kathleen Kinnaman from Decatur, Illinois, age twenty-three or so, unmarried. My grandfather's hair stood on end.

She almost married Sydney, a Jewish man she met in San Juan, but the story goes that Sydney's mother decisively blocked that from happening; no Illinois Methodists as daughters-in-law. So she came back from Puerto Rico and found herself another hospital dietician job on the Navajo Reservation in Ganado, way up in northwestern Arizona. My grandfather's hair continued to stand up, though her visits home must have been a comfort. The *Decatur Herald* reported on June 2, 1935: "Miss Kinnaman, daughter of Mr. and Mrs. B. O. Kinnaman, 175 Linden Place, arrived here last week from Sage Memorial hospital, Granada [*sic*], Ariz., where she has been dietician. The hospital is under the Presbyterian missions board and serves Navajo Indians."

In Ganado she met Bert. He had come to this corner of Arizona to work on civil engineering projects, probably irrigation. He and Kathleen were very different, he from a decidedly working-class New Mexico family, she a middle-class Midwesterner.

Kathleen Kinnaman in Ganado, Arizona, mid-1930s.

They were married in December of 1935 in her parents' living room in Decatur. We see her at her desk in 1934 or 1935 in her uniform, her dietician hat, and the engagement ring my father had given her. Her father's hair finally relaxed. Their first house on the reservation was a typical Navajo hogan with the door facing east.

The Lucases' hogan, 1935.

In making my mother a pair of moccasins, a Navajo woman was able to trace both of my mother's feet on one piece of paper. Her Navajo name thus became "Little Miss Two-Feet-on-One-Paper."

Among her possessions was a book entitled *Dineh Bizád—Navajo, His Language* compiled in 1932 by F. G. Mitchell and published in New York by the Board of National Missions of the Presbyterian Church in the U.S.A. *A Handbook for Beginners in the Study of the Navajo Language,* a slender, dark-red volume that starts with the alphabet and proceeds through word lists—greetings, travel, parts of the body, and on to conjugated verbs, including "to unhitch" and "to weave." A lot packed into 128 pages, including Navajo words for "church," "Christ," and "God," the latter being simply "God," a direct borrowing from English. In the very front, my mother wrote in her loopy handwriting, "Kathleen Kinnaman, Sage Memorial Hospital, October 1934."

As with many groups around the world, the Navajo use one word to mean both people in general and themselves specifically; the call themselves the Diné. Kathleeen had a tutor and tried to wade into the very intricate grammar and sound system. This is the language, after all, of the World War II code-talkers, the language that stumped the Japanese. I don't think she got very far, but her heart was clearly in the right place, recognizing there was a very long and deep culture surrounding her that she needed to learn something about.

Kathleen and Bert Lucas, 1980.

From Ganado, my parents made their way to Fort Defiance and Window Rock, Arizona, on to Green Mountain and Estes Park, Colorado, and finally to Phoenix in 1944, before leaving for Guatemala in 1956. For six of the early years in Arizona, Bert divided his time between Phoenix and Page, Arizona, where he worked on the Glen Canyon Dam. Kathleen taught sewing part-time at the so-called Indian School in Phoenix while tending to her daughters Jane (born in 1937) and Ellen Adonna (born in 1939). In 1948, they bought a home at 1530 W. Glenrosa, in what now has become central Phoenix. Following the social ethic for white middle-class women of the 1940s and 1950s, she worked only part-time after she got married and stopped completely when we moved to Guatemala. She was a registered dietician and also a very talented seamstress and teacher. I so dearly wish that she had worked full time until a normal retirement age to completely fulfill her potential, but it was not to be. How many times have I heard from friends and acquaintances, "Yeah, my dad told my mother that he didn't want her to work so she stopped." I don't know that my father ever said that, but the result was the same.

Kathleen Lucas in 1987.

March 1987: she is standing on the black volcanic sand of the beach in San Jose, Guatemala, the port on the Pacific side. She is a very well-put-together seventy-eight years old, six years a widow, my father having passed away in 1981. The plan was that he would finally retire, which he did at age sixty-nine, and that the two of them would then live out their lives together. They had started out in Arizona in 1935 and had bought a small retirement place amid the pines in Sunrise, east of Phoenix.

But it was not to be.

He passed very quickly of heart failure on July 20 of 1981, at age seventy-one. It was a Monday. "We said that we weren't going to do this!" she cried as we all looked at his body in the hospital room. Die before each other, that is.

But she very bravely soldiered on for eighteen more years: Elder Hostel in Asia, a return to Italy, a book group, reading books for the blind, tutoring English, finally being able to vote openly for Democrats—and enjoying the company of so many other widows. And this return to Guatemala. None of us had been back since May of 1960, and Guatemala was simply a place on a map for twenty-seven years. But now she wanted to go back.

It was 1987, and Guatemala would be in the grip of a military government for another nine years; ironically, it was quite safe to drive around the country. So she and I rented a car for a week and drove around to all our old haunts, including San Josè. I now understand the look in her eye, the unmistakable widow's look.

THE ITALY YEARS

The Square Colosseum

Italy and Rome in 1960 were the Italy and Rome of fifteen years after the end of World War II. That war brought the Italian economy to its knees—a peninsula with evidence of settlement and civilization by humans for at least six thousand years was reduced in many places to the level of a developing country. A developing country containing the Colosseum, the Forum, and the Palatine Hill, the masterpieces of Michelangelo, da Vinci, and Dante, the ruins of Pompeii and Paestum, but struggling in 1946 to provide basic services to its people—a literate people with a vast cultural, artistic, and historical heritage—*un patrimonio storico*—that struggled in the first years after the war to find enough for everyone to eat every day.

King Victor Emmanuel III had abdicated May 9, 1946, just a year after the war ended, and with the threat of a civil war, his son and successor Umberto II—the "May king" because he served slightly over one month—called a constitutional referendum on June 2, 1946, to decide if Italy should remain a monarchy or become a republic. The republican side won 54 percent of the vote. All male members of the ruling House of Savoy were banned from entering Italy, a ban that was not repealed until 2002.

The US government was of course watching all this, its main concern being the threat of control by the Communists and the Socialists. Prime minister Alcide De Gasperi—in the position 1945–1953—visited the United States in January 1947 and returned with $150 million in much-needed aid. US secretary of state George C. Marshall threatened that aid would be cancelled if the Communists and Socialists came to power. This in the context of deteriorating US relations with the Russians in the aftermath of World War II and seven years before

Arbenz was pushed from power in Guatemala and the Shah installed in Iran, both with intervention from the US government.

In the first parliamentary elections of the new republic in April 1948—which John Dickie refers to as the Cold War's first major electoral battle in Italy—the Christian Democrats and their Liberal, Social Democratic, and Republican partners were strongly backed by the United States. The Christian Democrats won 48 percent of the vote and dominated Italian politics for almost fifty years.

The economic recovery that came to known as the "economic miracle" or the "boom" started in 1946 with industrial growth rates of more than 8 percent per year. As the *Encyclopedia Britannica* states, "Its most prominent industries, still in the northwestern industrial triangle, produced fashionable clothing (especially shoes), typewriters, refrigerators, washing machines, furniture, plastics, artificial fibers, sewing machines, inexpensive motor scooters and cars." Italian companies became known for their combination of elegant design and inexpensive production. A network of superhighways was constructed across the country. In under two decades, Italy went from being an agricultural backwater to one of the world's most dynamic nations. One of the most important characteristics of the boom was internal migration, as about a million people moved from the south to other regions between 1958 and 1963.

In 1960, World War II was not that remote. Working adults, now in their thirties, forties, and fifties, had had their childhoods irretrievably shaped by the Mussolini regime, the war, and the extreme hardship that it had brought.

It was to this Italy and Rome that we arrived on Monday September 12, the day after the 1960 Olympics ended. These were the Olympics of Wilma Rudolph with her three gold medals in sprint events on the track. She was acclaimed as "the fastest woman in the world." And the Olympics of Cassius Clay, who won boxing's light-heavyweight gold medal. He would come to be known as Muhammad Ali. Many venues had been built from one end of the city to the other to accommodate the athletes. A number of these venues were built in the area south of the center, an area known as EUR, Esposizione Universale Roma. The development of the area, begun in 1938, was intended to symbolize the achievements of Fascism, but the development didn't get very far before Mussolini was forced to step down in July of 1943, as the war took a very different direction than the one he had expected. A number of the buildings remain and are still in use, including the Palazzo della Civiltà del Lavoro, built between 1938 and 1943. The plan was for it to be the centerpiece for a world exhibition in 1942, a symbol of Fascism for the world. Its famous inscription, a salute to the citizens of the country, reads: *Un popolo di poeti di artisti di eroi di santi di pensatori di scienziati di navigatori di transmigratori*—a population of poets, artists, heroes, saints, thinkers, scientists, navigators and movers, this evidently in a salute to the first intercontinental flights. It is variously known as *Il Colosseo Quadrato*—the Square Colosseum—or, as we kids knew it, *Il Palazzo della Groviera*—the Swiss Cheese Building. And of course, my adolescent Italian friends added a number of insulting and vulgar nouns to the list, reciting them with great glee.

This was about apartment living, a change from the ranch-style house in Guatemala City, and looking back, my very strong preference would have been an apartment in downtown Rome, near Piazza Navona or in the Monteverde area or, ideally, on the Aventine Hill, very near to my father's office at the Food and Agriculture Organization of the United Nations. The windows in that building look out on the Circus Maximus and the Palatine Hill, with the Tiber River and its island in the distance. Upon our arrival September 12, we stayed at the Santa Prisca, a convent-turned-hotel, with nuns still occupying part of the building. It is on the south end of the Aventine, with a view of the Pyramid of Gaius Cestius, a member of the ruling class. His pyramid tomb was built after his death in 12 BC. We stayed at the Santa Prisca for three weeks, so my first Roman neighborhood was the Aventine, and I would have been quite happy staying there. The school bus made a stop near the hotel; I had classmates who lived in that neighborhood, and I failed to understand why we could not stay there.

Our first apartment was on the long and wide boulevard that leads from the boundary of Rome marked by the Aurelian Wall, near the Baths of Caracalla, to EUR—Viale Cristoforo Colombo. The hulking grey apartment building was on a cross street named for the Roman emperor Alessandro Severo. The apartment was completely furnished, as our household goods had not yet arrived, and a small balcony gave us a wide view of the working-class Garbatella section of the city. The building is still very much there. Something brand new was the cranky elevator required to get to our apartment. Via Alessandro Severo had the usual shops—the fruit and vegetable guy, a bakery, a coffee bar. The school bus made a stop along the Cristoforo Colombo.

But we moved on to EUR. For my New Mexico–bred father, Old World Rome bore no fascination for him at all as a place to reside. He had a strong preference for open spaces and an apartment as close to a one-story house as possible, so we ended up in a ground-floor apartment in a building two blocks from the Swiss Cheese Building (the ground floor apartment on the left in the photo following).

Viale Pasteur 5, 1960.

The address was Viale Luigi Pasteur 5—yes, *that* Pasteur, Luigi (Louis), the French chemist and microbiologist renowned for his discoveries of the principles of vaccination, microbial fermentation, and pasteurization. The neighborhood also included Viale dell'Astronomia (Astronomy Street), Viale della Fisica (Physics Street), Viale dell'Elettronica (Electronics Street), and streets named, for example, for Asia, Europe, America, Stendhal, and Chopin. Rome in general is known for its neighborhoods in which the streets share a theme—South American countries, Italian regions, Italian cities, and the street names of EUR decided to take a tack in the direction of science and modernism. At that time EUR was somewhat of an enclave for expats and UN employees. Other such enclaves were Due Pini and Vigna Clara in the north end of the city, mostly for military and embassy types.

Our apartment had a lovely balcony that ran the full length of the apartment on one side; the living room and bedroom ceiling-to-floor windows opened on to it. It was also very modern in that the heating system had been installed in the travertine floors of the apartments—except for ours, because we were on the ground floor, right above the basement storage rooms. Many of the residents kept their wine in these cool rooms, and it was feared that heat in our floor would damage the wine. So no heating arrangement in our floors. As a result, there were many winter mornings when the temperature in our apartment hovered around 30 degrees Fahrenheit. One memorable sound from the Rome years is that of two tall, light-green kerosene stoves being opened and filled and then moved to the living room and the hallway near the bedrooms.

For the huge move from Guatemala City to Rome, a whole household needed to be packed and shipped to another continent. Everything was wrapped and packed, beds and shelves broken down, clothing and bedding folded and stashed in boxes. The contents of the kitchen were of course packed—dishes, pots, pans, silverware, linens, glasses, and one peanut butter jar full to the brim with red chili powder and tightly sealed. My mother did not oversee every single moment of the packing, and this would prove to be crucial. She probably said in her kitchen Spanish, "Please pack everything in this room." The packers were Guatemalans who spoke no English.

Having been raised in New Mexico, my father was a lover of chili powder, the very hot kind. He grew up speaking Spanish and eating Mexican food—but not anything that Taco Bell would recognize. When we lived in Guatemala, he had managed to find some chili powder that met his standards up in the mountains near the town of Cobán. It was sold in large piles in the market, and we kept it in a re-purposed peanut butter jar. And it was incorporated into meals when appropriate for the four years that we were there.

In those days, one's belongings arrived at the Customs area of the Fiumicino airport in Rome. Other experienced expats were able to talk newcomers through the process of retrieving their boxes, which had come by boat. Our stuff sat inexplicably in the Customs area for several weeks in September of 1960 before we were finally able to bring it home. There were forms to sign, and there was a lot of talking. But the unpacking exercise finally began. The living room took shape with our furniture and Guatemalan rugs; the beds were assembled and made up with familiar linens and quilts; the credenza, table, and chairs appeared in the dining room; and the kitchen boxes were unpacked.

At one point, Quinta, an Italian woman who was helping my mother unpack the contents of the kitchen presented her with an empty peanut butter jar, still with its lid on and with a very faint residue of red powder inside. The woman was totally puzzled as to why we would have bothered to ship an empty jar all the way from Guatemala to Rome. My mother took a look at it and then burst out laughing: the Guatemalan packers had known exactly what they were handling; they had carefully emptied the chili powder into another container that they could take with them and then conscientiously packed the empty jar in a box with the rest of the kitchen items. All we could do was laugh and admire the discerning palate of the packers.

A huge advantage of the location was the five-minute walk to the new subway, la Metropolitana, that my father could ride straight to the Circo Massimo stop and the UN building. Other UN families lived in our building, and my playmates right from the beginning were from India and Brazil.

Soon after we moved in, my playmates and I organized an Olympics that included competitive hopscotch, tree-climbing, running, and ball-throwing, all carefully scored. The award ceremony bestowed on the participants gold, silver, and bronze medals made of construction paper. We played in English.

At noon on hot summer days, we took picnics to the empty lot across the field, long-since filled with an office building.

One of the pieces of American culture that our mothers wanted to maintain was the observance of Halloween. The first and second of

November were religious holidays in Italy, of course, being All Saints' Day and All Souls' Day, respectively, the latter being the day when families visited cemeteries and placed flowers on the graves of their deceased. And there was Carnevale in February with hugely elaborate costume parties and enormous plastic bags of confetti to be thrown at everyone in the days leading up to Ash Wednesday.

Playmates in front of Palazzo della Civiltà del Lavoro, 1960s.
(Ceil, *middle row, second from left*, holding young girl's arms).

But there was no October 31 tradition, and apartment living in EUR presented a challenge. The solution was to pile six or seven be-costumed children, mostly girls, into the back of our Volvo station wagon at the appointed hour and drive them around to the apartments of their families to pound on front doors and shout, "Trick or treat!" while collecting candy. More than once, alarmed Italian neighbors would crack open their doors to peer out and try to understand what might possibly be happening. We repeated this ritual for probably four years, until we considered ourselves to be too old. Halloween has now become a very popular holiday in Italy.

A similar challenge was presented by Thanksgiving. It is now possible to order roasted turkey breast as an entree in a restaurant or trattoria, but in the 1960s, it was almost impossible to purchase any kind of turkey in a butcher shop. In this case, the commissary located in the basement of the UN building came through, selling frozen turkeys imported from England, and Thanksgiving dinners were able to proceed, dubbed Il Giorno di Ringraziamento. Thanksgiving Day, with all the tales of what had taken place that day in 1621 in a very faraway place called Plymouth, Massachusetts. We took it on faith that we should be grateful for something.

In addition to playing around the Palazzo della Civiltà and on its steps, we took our roller skates—the ones that had to be strapped to the soles of one's heavy shoes with a key—to the plaza surrounding the Basilica dei Santi Pietro e Paolo near the apartment. The plaza was made entirely of travertine marble, and skating on it was very smooth, like skating on air.

The resident priest was not impressed, and his disgruntlement finally resulted in the scene played out on the last day we skated there with us fur ously skating as he ran after us, his black robe and belt flying in the breeze, shouting, "*Andatevene via subito e non tornate!*" (Leave immediately and don't come back!). We managed at least one last turn around the church.

And, of course, we had our bikes. I had received mine for Christmas of 1959 in Guatemala, a beautiful royal-blue girl's bike with the lowered crossbar, no bike helmet required. We explored every possible corner of EUR, often leaving the house right after we got home from school, around 4 p.m., returning home in time for dinner. Remarkable that our parents had absolutely no idea where we were for three to four hours at a time but never expressed any concern. In that sense, I guess that we were free-range children.

On one expedition to the east end of EUR, in the Laurentina section, we discovered some caves that had been converted into mushroom farms. We parked our bikes and explored the dark, musty domed caves. At the south end of EUR, we came upon an abandoned strip mall with open doors and explored the quiet empty halls. And in more than one park, we observed what I learned a bit later were prostitutes with their johns, doing what they do in broad daylight under oleander bushes that did not shield them at all from curious young eyes. All in relative silence. Used condoms and wads of toilet paper littered those parts of the parks. As preteens, we weren't quite sure what we had seen, but we somehow had the insight to not tell our parents about this part of our explorations.

Since two of my playmates were Indian, returning to the entrance hall of the apartment building meant being enveloped night after night in the delicious aromas of Indian dinner being cooked in their apartment across the hall from ours. The smell of Indian cooking has been a madeleine for me ever since, propelling me immediately back to that entrance hall. Now, it should be noted that while their household was purportedly a vegetarian one, when the wife became aware that my mother was cooking meat—pork chops, a roast—she would sneak across the hall to consume a substantial sample. My mother never revealed these secret outings.

Then there was the Luna Park, located on the edge of EUR. For five hundred lire—about seventy-five cents in the early 1960s—we could spend the afternoon on the roller coaster, le Montagne Russe (the Russian Mountains), the bumper cars, and the labyrinth and house of mirrors. There was also the Centrifuge, which entailed being pinned against the wall as the cylinder spun. It required keeping one's eyes fixed on one spot for the entire ride to avoid throwing up. There were carnies with their throwing contests and the five hundred lire covered an ice cream cone or a soda.

From Viale Pasteur 5, I was taken to ballet lessons for a short time on the other side of Rome. This was one more Italian-immersion experience, as I was the only English speaker in a group of twelve or so students. I also went on almost-yearly, week-long ski trips to Terminillo, Gstaad, Cervinia, and Val Gardena. And once on a disastrous two-week stay at an Appenine tennis camp in Sestola, near Modena. In that beautiful spot amidst pine trees, it became clear that I was not cut out to be a tennis player, much less any kind of star.

EUR and the apartment were home until I went away to college in August of 1969. My parents lived there until May of 1971, when they moved back to the United States for good. Eleven years at Viale Pasteur 5. The apartment is now a law firm.

"Piange"

About a month after we arrived in Rome, I was plunged into Italian head first, verbs and all. I came to Rome fully armed with Spanish, and I was taking Italian classes at school, of course. The walkway into our apartment building was covered by an awning. At the end of it was a very modern front door made of glass with metal sculptures on it, and the custodian's desk was tucked into a corner of the lobby. He and his family had an apartment in the basement, and he was usually out and about tending to various repairs and general upkeep of the building.

But on this day, he was seated at his desk and of course greeted me. It had started to rain lightly and when I saw the custodian, I exclaimed to him, "Piange!" which means that someone, male or female, is crying.

He looked at me with a quizzical and slightly concerned look, as if he would spring into action if need be, and asked, "*Chi piange?*" ("Who is crying?"). I stopped for a moment and then said, "*Piove*" ("It's raining"), with a sheepish look on my face. He walked to the door to verify my claim.

In her autobiography, *Lessico famigliare*, the Italian author Natalia Ginzburg says of her mother that many of her memories were directly linked to language—words or phrases that had struck her, inevitably surrounded by a story—"*Molti dei suoi ricordi erano così: semplici frasi che aveva sentito.*" (Many of her memories were like that: simple phrases that she had heard.) For example, a young schoolgirl walking in a line with her classmates in Turin in the 1930s recognizes the littermate of her dog while walking down the street and runs to hug it, exclaiming with the features of regional Italian, "*L'è le, l'è le, l'è la sorella della mia cagna!*" ("It's her, it's her, the sister of my she-dog!")

My memory works the same way. So many language-based recollections, as far back as I can remember. I have always been a listener and a language learner and continue to be one. This moment with the custodian momentarily exposed the language learning process that was usually totally below the level of awareness, at least for me, for the four languages that I had learned by the time I was ten. It showed that I was actively working on my language and communication skills, as I was clearly eager to provide the custodian with an accurate meteorological report.

The process was totally exposed when, at age forty-two, I started to learn Irish. Books, tapes, classes, and nowhere near enough immersion for the process to disappear. It did disappear a lot when I started to learn American Sign Language at age thirty-one, but I was immersed, could see as much ASL as I wanted every day. A curiosity about language that started in Guatemala in 1956 and that continues.

Long White Objects

In 1960 in Italy, it was still possible to buy single cigarettes. They each cost under fifty lire, about eight American cents, and were the national brand, Nazionali—no filter, just your basic cigarette. They were presented to the buyer in a small paper bag. This was without doubt a reflex of the very tough war years during which hardly anyone could afford a whole pack and certainly not American cigarettes. Marlboros and other American brands were highly prized starting with the American presence in 1943 and were still so in 1960. In 1967, my half-Italian, half-Belgian boyfriend openly coveted my father's Kents.

I met my friend in September of 1960. She lived in an apartment building across the street from ours, and every day for eight years, we rode the same bus to our school, an hour away on the north side of Rome. She had two younger brothers. The youngest one was routinely late for the bus, leading to the whole bus-full of children and teenagers yelling out the windows up to the apartment, "The bus!" while Signor Valli patiently waited.

In addition to riding the bus together every day, my friend and I spent hours of free time together over about six years. We explored our neighborhood, listened to music, talked about boys and clothes, the usual. I was occasionally invited to the beach club where we spent entire days swimming and playing on the beach. And one day, we decided to satisfy our curiosity about cigarettes, which we saw many adults smoking—in 1960, still mostly men.

On that particular outing, we were probably thirteen, and we had been compelled by my friend's mother to take her youngest brother with us. We ventured into the tobacco store, where one also bought stamps and salt, and purchased two single cigarettes. The matches were free. We said that we were buying for one of our fathers, and no questions we asked. We headed off to a park near our apartment buildings and got settled under a large bush. My friend lit one of the cigarettes and we both tried it, puffing and coughing. We both found it disgusting, ended the experiment, and headed home.

As soon as my friend and her brother got home, their mother realized from the smell what we had been up to and demanded an explanation. My friend of course denied any wrongdoing, but when pressed, her brother said, "Well, they took some long white objects, put them in their mouths, and lit them."

My mother was immediately called and appropriate talking-tos were administered. The little brother proudly maintained that he had never actually snitched, that he had never actually said, "They smoked cigarettes." We were furious, but he felt entirely justified. His precocious use of language was impressive.

Quinta

With the extremely graceful Italian euphemism for saying someone has died, the email states, *"Nonna Quintilia [è] venuta a mancare"* ("Grandmother Quintilia has come to be missing.") The auxiliary verb is curiously left out. The euphemism leaves room for hope that the person will reappear, that she has simply wandered off and will be back within a reasonable amount of time. But no, Quinta—as we knew her—was gone for good. The email is dated August 21, 2005, and was sent by the younger of her two sons, Renato, now in his late sixties. The oldest is Enzo, early seventies, and there is a daughter as well, Daniela, a couple of years younger than I am, early sixties.

Quinta Bucci in her early twenties.

Quinta cleaned our apartment at Viale Pasteur 5, every two weeks for eleven years. When we moved into the building, other tenants quickly told my mother, "You need Quinta. We'll have her come talk to you when she's done today." She added us to her list of clients immediately. She swept, mopped, dusted, washed the clothes, hung them on the roof—no dryer available at that time—and retrieved them. She was extremely thorough.

We lived in the south end of the city. She lived with her family due east of us, in the working-class Centocelle section. Due east, with no direct public transportation in those days; she had to take two buses, requiring two hours each way through Roman traffic. This explained why her clients were all in the three apartment buildings that made up our little compound.

She was a native speaker of the Roman variety of Italian and spoke no English at all. She and my mother figured how to communicate with a limited vocabulary list—I'm pretty sure that there wasn't much syntax being produced—and for me, Quinta became yet one more model of colloquial Italian. We only and always spoke Italian to each other. My name is not far from the Italian word for sky, *cielo*, and that immediately was the name she gave me, spoken with the Roman accent—where the *ch* becomes *sh* so *shehlo* and "*Ah, Sheh!*" in the vocative form. That's what her sons and everyone in their extended families still call me. Her husband had the most Roman surname possible, Proietti (as common as Smith in the United States), but Italian women keep their family names when they marry, and hers was Bucci. I always called her Quinta, never Signora Bucci.

Quintilia Bucci was born in 1919 in the town of Gerano, east of Rome in the Lazio region. She had made her way to Rome in search of a better life and was twenty years old when World War II started. Her education was limited to fifth or sixth grade. Enzo was born in the devastated Rome of 1944 when Quinta was twenty-five.

She told stories of making winter shoes for him and his brother Renato out of cardboard and string. And she told a story of Piuccio, *un mezzo parente*—a sort of relative—who wanted to borrow her brother's bicycle, a relative luxury during the war.

Piuccio said, "Look, if you lend me the bicycle, I'll give you ten kilos of flour." And the exchange took place.

Quinta in 1996, age seventy-seven.

Quinta notes that she immediately made fresh pasta. "And I know how to make fresh pasta !" And somehow she came up with two to-matoes—in dialect, *du pomodori*—to make a sauce. But as they started eating the pasta, they discovered that what had been given to them as flour was marble dust, completely inedible—"*Mangiavi e sentivi 'crak crak.*'" ("You ate and heard 'crack crack.'")—so it all had to be thrown out. She goes on to stress that she was sure that Piuccio did not know what he had given them because he wouldn't treat relatives in that way.

So the war years were very rough for Quinta and her family, but by 1960, things were looking up. She and her husband, an electrician, lived in a newly built apartment building and owned a car; there was a small garden of vegetables and flowers. Still, it was Italy in the 1960s. She told of working all day and of arriving home after a two-hour bus ride to find her husband and two adolescent sons sitting sullenly at the dining room table waiting for dinner to be served. Not one of them had put a pot of water on the stove to cook the pasta; not one had set the table or put the bread in a basket. So, after eight hours of physical labor bracketed by a four-hour round trip commute, she would prepare dinner. Dinner for the husband who, at one point, saw fit to step out of the marriage. No legal divorce for anyone in Italy until 1970, so she soldiered on, seething.

My friendship with Quinta lasted until her death. I saw her every time I went to Italy between 1976 and 2005 and frequently stayed with her. I have kept in touch with her sons and their children and see them during visits to Rome, usually sharing very loud and hilarious meals filled with reminiscences of our childhoods and long and deep discussions about politics in Italy and the United States.

Quinta provided a very early, powerful, and enduring model for me of how a very moral and kind life can be lived, despite serious economic deprivation and a rough start. I obviously found truths with her that I did not find at home. Her formal education was fairly limited—she could read and write—but her mind was very sharp, and she had a clear understanding of human nature with all its angles.

She was able to help me through difficult times in my life, like a divorce—something that was not that easy to discuss with my parents. She had a wicked sense of humor, and we laughed on more than one occasion until we both had tears running down our cheeks, usually at the absurdities and foibles of our fellow humans.

And she was a direct link to Rome—its language, its culture, its food, the Rome of Romans, not of tourists. My friendship with her helped define my Rome. By the end of her life, she had a comfortable retirement. She owned her apartment and had inherited the family home in Gerano, which she visited quite regularly, bringing back homemade wine and fresh produce. Her knees, blown out by forty-five years of scrubbing floors and carrying bins of wet laundry, were successfully replaced. She never did learn how to drive and never traveled beyond Sicily and Sardinia. There was talk of her visiting my mother in the United States, plans that were never realized.

As a sophomore in college, age nineteen, I decided that I needed a job to earn some money, as opposed to having all of it handed to me by my parents. I got a job cleaning three houses in Walla Walla. My three employers were an elderly couple, a widow, and one of the rich be-mansioned leaders of the community. Over the 1970–71 academic year, I cleaned each house every two weeks, dusting, vacuuming, mopping, doing laundry. I came away with cash and a sense of accomplishment. I voluntarily cleaned houses. My mother was certainly not the inspiration for this choice.

THE OVERSEAS SCHOOL OF ROME

I started at the Overseas School of Rome the third week of September 1960. In his book, *An American in Rome*, Michael Stern describes how his wife and a woman named Sylvia Horwitz, who also had a school-age son, conceived of the idea of starting a school for US and other foreign dependents. A general Charlie Dasher was approached. Since a lot of real estate in Rome was under US Army control in 1946, General Dasher said, "I'd like to make a deal with you. . . . The families of our military personnel are beginning to arrive. We expect quite a number of them. If your school will accept the children of our dependents, I'll not only give you the building, but I'll also let you have as many school supplies as I can lay my hands on. And if I find any teachers in our ranks, I'll also help with the staff."

Stern goes on to say, "Thus was born the Overseas School of Rome, today [1964] one of the largest private schools in the country, ranking high scholastically and socially." It was incorporated in 1947 and first occupied the palazzetto of Villa Torlonia, located on Via Nomentana, in the east and slightly north section of the city. It moved to its Via Cassia location, on the north edge of the city, in 1952, the student body "reflecting the increased numbers of parents assigned to embassies, consulates, and the United Nations, or living in Rome as scholars, artists, journalists, and professionals."

The school website offers this information: "Five American and five British mothers . . . got together and decided to form a school that would be non-denominational and international, and would combine the best of the British and American systems. This original group of mothers is responsible for the organization of the official corporation that became our school."

Overseas School of Rome villa, 1960s.

Overseas School of Rome elementary school, 1960s.

Overseas School of Rome high school and gym, 1960s.

The original building was a three-story villa located in the middle of the property. The elementary school and high school buildings were slowly added, along with the Hillside Theatre. One lovely feature of the original school was that the kindergarten and first grade classrooms were located on the same quadrangle with the upper elementary grades, so the older children were around the younger ones and sometimes helped out with them.

The school is now known as AOSR, the *A* for American, and the student population now stays around 630.

I came from Guatemala armed with *A Child's History of the World*, full of Greek, Roman, and medieval history, and now found myself at the epicenter of a lot of this history. Rome and its environs constituted a vast supplemental classroom: field trips to the Forum, the Palatine and the Circus Maximus, the Colosseum, the Pantheon, Piazza Navona, the Palatine and Lateran Museums, the Vatican and its museums, the catacombs, Hadrian's Villa and Tivoli, walks around downtown Rome, Castelgandolfo, Frascati, and other sites in the hills south of the city, and as we got older, trips to the Fosse Ardeatine, the site of the Nazi atrocities against the Roman Jewish community in March of 1944. We were taken on overnight school trips to Venice, Verona, Florence, Pompeii, and Herculaneum with faculty chaperones who may still be recovering.

We were taught European history—but, curiously, almost no American history at all. We dutifully memorized and recited lists of the capitals of American states—Montpelier, Vermont; Pierre, South Dakota; Concord, New Hampshire—but could not have found any of them on a map. Many of us could tell you the borders of all European countries and the borders of the Italian regions, but the map of America remained a mostly theoretical proposition.

I do remember preparing a book report on a book about a Native American tribe, which I had read and researched in the school library. It was there that I found biographies of Clara Barton and George Washington Carver, among many others, in a biographical series with orange covers.

We were well versed in international current events through Italian newspapers and some television and magazines like *Time* and the English-language newspaper, the *Daily American*—later made famous by the John Prine song based on the Dear Abby advice column that appeared in it. But, given the sheer enormity of what was happening in the United States between 1956 and 1968 with, for example, the civil rights movement, the Vietnam War and the opposition to it, and presidential politics, it is sobering to realize that my awareness of all of that was pretty limited.

There was of course extensive coverage of the murders of John and Bobby Kennedy and Martin Luther King Jr. in eighth grade and senior year—and I remember how very deeply affected the American faculty and recently arrived students were by all three—but for many of us, it remained fairly remote. For me, it became a matter of self-education starting in 1969 when I went to the United States for college and continuing after August 1972, following the move back.

We ventured into fifth grade arithmetic, with word problems about trains leaving different cities at given times and X miles per hour and when would they encounter each other on the tracks, and many worksheets for homework. Geometry, algebra, intro to biology, intro to physics, English, American, and European literature, much of the latter in the original languages, history, world religions, Latin, Italian, French.

So we made our way through the usual elementary education and on into and through middle school and high school.

Our apartment was in EUR, in the south end of the city, and OSR was on the north edge. This entailed a daily bus ride, one full hour each way through traffic along the west and northwest side of the city; we crossed the Tiber going and coming. A huge green oil refinery located near the Monte Verde section—and now long gone, replaced with apartment complexes—belched smoke smelling of sulphur as we passed. In the mornings, we watched adults walking and driving to work and children being escorted to school, the youngest ones in their smocks—*grembiuli*—with great ribbons at their necks. The boys generally wore black or blue smocks, while the girls' were pink. We watched as the stores opened, fruit and vegetable vendors getting their produce out on sidewalk stands; we watched as people consumed their first espresso or cappuccino in neighborhood bars. The bus route took us through a decidedly residential and business area of the city, nothing of interest for tourists but a very clear picture of daily life in ordinary Rome.

Overseas School of Rome bus, 1960s.

We of course completed most of our homework during the hour-long ride home, except for the math word problems, but the bus was also a rolling microcosm of life at the school—children from all over the world, including Italian kids and teenagers beginning to explore the hierarchies of high school politics and also necking in the very back seats to the deep fascination of the younger kids and the full annoyance of the bus driver, Mr. Valli.

The elementary school music room was located at the end of a long row of classrooms that looked out on the courtyard that had several Roman pines in it. Grades 2 through 6, each with an A and a B, so ten classrooms and the boys' and girls' bathrooms and the nurse's office. The kindergartners and first graders were on the other side of the courtyard. Returning to the school for the first time after high school graduation in May of 1968, I had the classic Alice in Wonderland experience, as the row of classrooms and the courtyard seemed to have dramatically shrunk; I felt like a giant.

The music room was large, with one whole wall consisting of windows that faced the Via Cassia. We could see the school buses lined up in the parking lot. At one end of the room was a small upright piano and a chair to go with it. There were no desks in the room, only student-sized chairs with plastic backs. Bookshelves filled with books about music and composers hugged the wall opposite the windows. There was plenty of space on one of the walls for student drawings to be hung. The music teacher was Mrs. Barbara Sparti, an American married to an Italian. I think that we trooped to her classroom at least once and maybe twice a week for music instruction. It was a combination of music appreciation and learning songs from the American songbook. Very occasionally, we would play percussion instruments in accompaniment of her piano playing or a record.

The music appreciation part introduced us to well-known classical works. Most memorable was the day that we each illustrated a different section of Mussorgsky's *Pictures at an Exhibition* and then acted out our illustrations—the Great Gate at Kiev, The Gnome, The Old Castle, Goldenberg and Schmuyle—whom I envisioned as a large fat man and his small, skinny companion making their way along the street, Laurel and Hardy. The illustrations were done with crayons on butcher paper and then displayed on the wall for all to see. One result: I have loved that piece of music since 1960 and have gone on to love the whole world of classical music—up to about 1930. With a few exceptions like Benjamin Britten and Samuel Barber, I run out of patience with modern composers right after Stravinsky. Patience or not, Mrs. Sparti opened the door and pushed us through. And then there was the American songbook. I don't know if she was told to use this or did it on her own, but the result was that a whole passel of expat children was introduced to American history and culture through song: "She'll be Comin' Round the Mountain," "My Darling Clementine," "Goober Peas," "Home on the Range," "I've Been Working on the Railroad," "Deep in the Heart of Texas," "Way Down upon the Swanee River," "Davy Crockett," all accompanied on the piano by Mrs. Sparti. The songs referred to places that were very vague in all our minds, but we sang our hearts out, as though we had known where the American South and Texas were all along. And, when the season rolled around, we sang American Christmas songs. She always played the piano standing up, so as to direct our singing. We were given a cardboard folder with metal clips in it where we could keep the lyrics.

Hansel and Gretel, 1967–1968 (Ceil on far left).

Scenes from *Macbeth*, 1968 (Ceil in the middle).

We also participated in productions of Gilbert and Sullivan oper-
ettas and American musicals—*The Gondoliers*, *The Mikado*, *Oklahoma!*,
Guys and Dolls. I was cast as Tessa in *The Gondoliers* in the fall of 1960
and mercifully discovered at age nine that, even though I was strongly
drawn to theatre, my true skills were as a stage manager and a lifelong
audience member and not as a performer. I did turns as Aunt Eller
in *Oklahoma!*, General Cartwright in *Guys and Dolls*, the mother in
Engelbert Humperdink's *Hansel and Gretel*, and a pregnant dung beetle
in Karel and Joseph Čapek's *The Insects*—obsequious and self-serving,
the dung beetle—but was much more comfortable tending to the costumes and the sets.

Mrs. Sparti directed the elementary school productions, and the
high school ones were handled by the astonishing Argentine music
teacher, Mr. Silvio Estrada, who would accompany and conduct each
performance standing at the piano located in front of the stage. These
musicals, especially the American ones, were part of the window on
America being provided for those of us who were not quite sure where
Oklahoma or the New York of Damon Runyon might be. We did peri-
odic Shakespeare festivals and poetry competitions, which involved the

recitation of parts of plays and poems, but that was Shakespeare and a lot of European poetry. American musicals came from somewhere else.

I went to Mrs. Sparti's music class only for fifth and sixth grades, 1960–1962; in seventh grade, we moved on. Some of my classmates had come to the school several years before me and had thus benefited from her instruction since first or second grade. I wonder how Mrs. Sparti's choice of music changed after Bob Dylan and Joan Baez, the Beatles and the Rolling Stones came along. Motown was already on the scene. Students in her class from 1960–1962 would not have been exposed to the American songbook without her. Whether she knew it or not, she filled in a huge gap that most of us had—and filling it in prepared us in some small way for lives in the faraway America.

Mrs. Sparti passed away in 2013 at age eighty-one. By the time of her passing, she had built a career as an authority on medieval and renaissance dance, known worldwide. Strangely, the obituaries and tributes make no mention whatsoever of her years at OSR, years that were so foundational to so many of us.

Along with the American musicals, there was a concerted effort by the American parents and school administrators to expose us as much as possible to aspects of American culture and American school life. Most of these American parents and school administrators had come to Rome as adults; they had been raised in the United States and had come up through the American high school experience and clearly felt that this experience should be shared as much as possible with the OSR students. They were also very aware that most of the students would return to the United States to complete their high school education or for college, so they needed to be acculturated and prepared.

Organized sports teams and cheerleading squads were, and are, non-existent in Italian schools at any level; the fierce rivalries between high school, college, and university teams are completely absent. But OSR had a cheerleading squad for the basketball team. Becoming a cheerleader involved a very competitive audition process; a number of friendships were lost in the process. Now, it must be said that the teams from the various American base schools—Naples, Livorno (known to the American kids as Leghorn), Verona, Vicenza—quite regularly mopped the floor with our team, so it was never clear if the cheerleaders had any effect, but they had enviable maroon and white uniforms, very short skirts and jaunty vests, spotless white socks and tennis shoes. They of course had to shave their legs and wear make-up. They traveled on the bus to away games.

We had both a junior and a senior prom, usually held at one of the fancy hotels in Rome. No yearbooks to be found in Italian high schools, but we produced the *Tabularium*, an American-style yearbook that included photos of students from the middle school up and a record of the theatrical productions, the literary journal, and all the various after-school clubs—chess, French, physics. Securing autographs on graduation day was paramount.

Some of us attended the MAAG movies in the annex of the American embassy. This was the Military Assistance Advisory Group, and they showed American movies on Friday nights and Saturday afternoons. We paid twenty-five American cents to get in, with one hundred lire for popcorn. In the mid-1960s, we saw black-and-white World War II films—*Strategic Air Command, None but the Brave*, and others—and again, as on the school bus, watched in fascination as the older kids necked in the back rows of the balcony.

And last but not least, there was the Sears catalog, appearing twice a year during our stay in Rome, mid-spring and fall, the latter in time for Christmas orders. We never ordered that much, but its thin pages were studied as if it were an anthropology textbook. It was full of American people and things, many of which we had never seen before—farm and garden implements, guns and their accessories, toys, electronic equipment as it was in the 1960s, all manner of household items, and men, women, and children in their underwear. It was like a popular encyclopedia of American life, mid-1960s. White American life; I don't remember any models of color at all.

We were fed lunch every day at the school. The cafeteria was in the basement of the main building, a vast room with a stage at one end, the site for the American musicals. Ceiling-to-floor windows with some doors ran the full length of the west side. During lunch, there were long folding tables and folding chairs for probably two hundred students. Lunch was served at noon, an hour earlier than in most Italian households. And it was cooked by a wonderful collection of Roman ladies who tried to accommodate the palates of children and adolescents from all over the world—Americans, Brits, Italians, Jordanians, Ethiopians, Turks, you name it. They mostly succeeded.

The pasta dishes were okay, but they didn't always translate to the large quantities needed. Someone, perhaps one of the British founders of the school, had convinced the kitchen staff that shepherd's pie—a ghastly mix of mashed potatoes and ground beef—would be good. It was a disaster, but no weekly menu was ever posted, so when it showed up, it was either eat it or go hungry.

I don't remember being given milk cartons—which thoroughly enchanted me the two times that I very briefly attended American schools when we went to the United States for home leave. But I do remember that dessert was always fruit—never cookies or cakes, ever—but in Rome, with astonishing peaches, pears, figs, and grapes, and tart green and red apples in the fall, we never missed it. The politics of the cafeteria were universal—who sat with whom, who was the current object of gossip and derision. After lunch, we would sit out on the hill behind the cafeteria—now the site of the Hillside Theatre—taking in the Roman sun like lizards on a warm rock.

Il Campeggio Inca

In the 1960s, the headquarters of the YMCA in Rome was located in a non-descript office building on Piazza Indipendenza, adjacent to the main train station. The YMCA offered two-week sessions at a beach camp in Olbia in northeast Sardinia. The director of the YMCA in Italy at that time was Olindo Parachini.

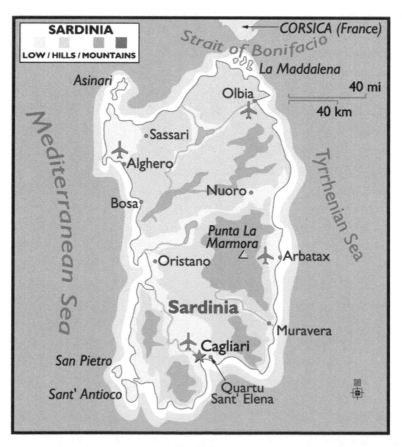

Sardegna.

Olindo was born in Piemonte in 1919 in the town of Varallo Pombia, just south of Lago Maggiore and very close to Switzerland to the north and France to the west. His family moved to France when he was six months old, and he was raised speaking French. However, since he had been born in Italy, he was pressed into military service there in 1941. At the end of the war in 1945, he was hired by the Red Cross to help relocate Italians from hospitals and mental wards and was then hired by the YMCA in Belgium and worked there until 1959. He met his wife in Belgium, and both of his children—a son and a daughter—were born there. In January of 1959, he became the Secretario Generale, director, of the YMCA in Rome and stayed there until he retired in 1979.

In the summer of 1959, a YMCA camp was established on an empty beach property on the outskirts of Olbia, with US Army surplus tents and twenty-five children in attendance, seven children and a leader to a tent. By 1960, a dining hall and kitchen had been built, and the lavatories were expanded.

The top image in the following pair of photos shows the camp as of 1964 with the lavatories, not visible, located to the right. The bottom photo shows the camp in the 1970s and 1980s with the addition of a second floor to the kitchen—sleeping quarters for the kitchen help. The ancient lighthouse can be seen in the background. The area is still known as Lido del Sole—beach of the sun. I call it the Campeggio Inca because of the Italian pronunciation of YMCA. The separate letters are not pronounced as they are in English; the whole acronym becomes a word and by being located between the high front vowel *i* (the *Y* in YMCA) and the high back consonant *k* (the *C* in YMCA), the *M* never stood a chance. It almost immediately disappeared from its bilabial position into the mouth and came to be pronounced as ŋ, a velar consonant like *k*, the final sound in the English words king or sing—hence, Inca—the Sardinian camp with the Peruvian-sounding name.

Trasformazioni

YMCA camp, Olbia (ymcatime.blogspot.com).

We got to the camp on a bus from Piazza Independenza to the port
of Civitavecchia, about fifty miles north of Rome on the coast, via the
Aurelia highway. We then took an overnight ferry that arrived in Olbia
at seven in the morning. Accommodations on the ferry were large re-
clining chairs. We were always too excited to sleep and gathered on the
deck to watch the entry into the port. We were assigned to our tents in
one of two groups—juniors and seniors.

We wore shorts and T-shirts; I took my shoes off when we arrived
at the camp and put them back on only for short trips away from the
camp and for the journey home.

Meals were taken in the dining room—*mensa*—the largest building on the property—a light Mediterranean breakfast of bread, butter,

jam, and warm milk with a splash of coffee, a full lunch with pasta, meat, and vegetables, and following the two-hour siesta, a late afternoon snack consisting of a bowl of hot tea and a hollow roll—*rosetta*—with a small bar of chocolate to be placed inside it. Following afternoon activities, dinner was again light—bread, cheese, cold cuts, fruit.

Daily activities revolved around the water and the beach—swim lessons and swimming contests, diving from the platform that was situated about one hundred yards from the beach and required good swimming skills. There were *lavori manuali*, arts and crafts sessions in which we drew, painted, and made putty sculptures incorporating shells.

Tent at YMCA camp, Olbia, 1960s.

There were day-long hikes to Porto Istana, a small bay south of the camp with completely unspoiled water. Lunch on these hikes involved again opening a rosetta and emptying a small can of potted meat into it, brand name Simmenthal, actually very delicious. We were also taken by bus to the Costa Smeralda on the north end of Sardinia, pristine in the early 1960s and soon taken over by the properties of the Aga Khan and Berlusconi.

At night, there were dances in the mensa, variety shows consisting of skits put together by the campers and the leaders, bonfires and singing, and the adaptation of the snipe hunts carried out at American camps.

On special occasions, there were excursions to the beach bar down the road from the camp. The bar had a jukebox, so we drank soft drinks and danced to contemporary Italian pop music until we ran out of change.

We also explored the old lighthouse, which could be seen from the camp—we, of course, had to race to the top of it for the view—and the World War II cement bunker, located right outside the camp.

This was my first exposure to summer camp, and I was enchanted with the beach and the swimming and the tents. But what would turn out to be most important was my total immersion in Italian at the camp. We had been in Italy since September of 1960, and I first went to the camp in the early summer of 1961. By that point, I had had an academic year of Italian courses and had started on lifelong friendships that took place entirely in Italian, but the YMCA camp experience sealed the deal. There were some other American children at the camp when I was there, but I have no memory at all of any conversations in English.

German WW II bunker near YMCA camp, Olbia, with a lighthouse in the background (courtesy Alessandro Borrini).

In the summer of 1961, my leader was from Rome and all the girls in my tent were also Romans. It was at this point, at age ten, that I nailed down the subjunctive, conditional, imperfect, and imperative moods, added massively to my vocabulary, got indirect and direct object pronouns firmly in place, along with all the other myriad and essential details of the language, all without giving the process any thought at all. In the parlance of those who study child language, I simply acquired the language and learned to use it appropriately with the pragmatics of conversational use and the formal and informal forms of address properly in order. And as part of it, I started to lay down my Roman accent, quite distinct from the accents of other regional varieties of Italian—again, without thinking about it. I simply learned the variety of where I had been planted with an accent as distinct as the accent of a Boston or Chicago or Brooklyn native. I wouldn't have changed it if I could, but at that point, I had no choice in the matter.

It was somewhat later that I developed my awareness of the centrality of accents and dialects in Italy and my appreciation for Roman poets and writers, such as Trilussa (Carlo Alberto Salustri, his pen name being an anagram of his last name) and Giuseppe Gioachino Belli, with their wry, always self-deprecating and ironic take on Roman life and their enormous affection for their language. There were also many Roman drinking songs, *stornelli*, proverbs and colloquial expressions to be learned and applied. *"Ma lui è romano?"* ("Is he Roman?"), someone would ask. *"E più de così se more!"* ("If you're more Roman than that, you're dead!") would be the response. *"Hai visto che traffico a Roma con la pioggia?"* ("Did you see the traffic in Rome with the rain?"), to which the answer is *"A voja!,"* which means roughly "don't you wish" but is pronounced so it sounds like *avoya* (yup, or you got it). *"Ma hai mangiato tutta quella pasta?"* ("You ate all that pasta?") contested with *"Ce vo'!"* ("One has to!), the standard Italian phrase *ci vuole* (it's necessary), with the *ch* sound of *ci* realized as the unmistakable *sh* sound and the verb reduced from *vuole* to *vo*. The *l* sound in *soldato* (soldier), *soldi* (money), and other words becomes an *r*, *sordato*, *sordi*. And consonants are routinely doubled, so that *sabato* (Saturday) sounds like *sabbato*. I was about thirty—watching the ad with the "I Can't Believe It's Not Butter" guy—when I first realized that the man's name Fabio is spelled with one *b*, not Fabbio, as it is pronounced in Rome. In short, I ingested completely a regional variety of Italian and also acquired the deep feelings of pride and affection about it.

Years later as an adult professional starting to do academic presentations in Italy, I had the extremely rude awakening that my Roman accent and colloquial manner of speaking might not be considered at all appropriate for formal settings—the colloquial manner probably wouldn't have been acceptable in any academic setting in any country—and I had to adjust my repertoire in very short order. I had been teaching standard Italian to undergraduates and adults for ten years by the time I started doing professional presentations in Italy, and I'm sure that I was faithful to the language textbooks I was using and exposed the students to standard Italian. I had also been studying sociolinguistics for those same ten years and was forming a very clear picture of the prestige varieties of a language, as opposed to non-prestige ones—of which the Roman variety is usually given as an example—so a scholarly context had been set up in my consciousness for my Roman variety. But I had never done presentations for adult native speakers of the language in formal settings. My Roman sound system could not be hidden, and I heard about it. I also responded somewhat defensively, the Roman pride slightly wounded. But my solid fluency in the language could not be denied, the seeds of that fluency having been planted in the fall of 1960 and nurtured intensively in Sardinia starting in 1961.

The foundation was also laid for an inside attachment to Rome and Italy, as opposed to that of a tourist. The monuments, the famous food and wine, the weather, yes. But starting with the Campeggio Inca and continuing with other interactions and experiences soon to follow, I started to move behind the external stereotypes and images of Rome and Italy perceived by the world and into the life of real Italians. I acquired an Italian affection for both city and country, started to understand values and perceptions that distinguish Italians, including perceptions of foreigners. The affection for the country was built by the extensive travel that my parents and I did in the eleven years that we were there together—of course, Florence for the Easter Sunday celebrations; Venice, Pompeii, Siena, Perugia, Genova, Sorrento, the Amalfi Coast, and Paestum, all car trips—but also the north on our way to ski weeks in Switzerland, Calabria, the Gargano Peninsula, and Puglia; on our way to Brindisi and the ferry to Greece; east to the Abruzzo region and the hinterlands of the Lazio region of Rome. Sicily would wait until the spring of 1972.

I ended up being voted *Campeggista dell'anno* (Camper of the Year) in 1961, despite a short bout of stomach flu that led to me barfing spectacularly out the window of the canvas tent—I had reasoned that I wouldn't be able to make it down from the top bunk and out the door in time. Campeggista dell'anno despite, or maybe because of, my bravery in the face of illness. I was awarded a certificate at the fall reunion dinner. I was not at all alarmed by having been sick, but it freaked my mother out completely, and I was sent the following year, 1962, to an American Girl Scout camp on Lake Garda near the American air force base in Verona.

Ceil in Girl Scout uniform, about age twelve.

Somewhere between Guatemala City and Rome, I had moved up from Brownie to Girl Scout, with its motto, "be prepared," explained as "A Girl Scout is ready to help out wherever she is needed. Willingness to serve is not enough; you must know how to do the job well, even in an emergency."

More tents, much more expensive ones, s'mores, sit-upons made of cotton cloth and oil cloth with ribbons to tie them around our waists, a thoroughly American diet, all conversations in English. No beach. Mercifully, I think it lasted only seven days. The "be prepared" part definitely stuck and, like it or not, was a major guideline during a career of teaching and research.

So by now, it's 1967. In the summers of 1964 and 1966, we were on home leave in the United States, and I'm not sure how I passed the time in the summers of 1963 and 1965. I do know that in the spring of 1967 I rode the metro down to the YMCA headquarters and marched into Olindo Parachini's office. I asked to be assigned to the camp as a leader to the summer session. I was sixteen. We addressed each other with informal pronouns. On many other occasions, we spoke French, but this time, it was Italian with informal pronouns:

Ceil: *"Voglio lavorare come leader quest'estate, e vorrei occuparmi dei lavori manuali."* ("I want to work as a leader this summer, and I would like to be in charge of the arts and crafts.")

Olindo: *"Ma i leader devono avere almeno diciassette anni."* ("But the leaders have to be at least seventeen years old.")

Ceil: *"Ma sono pronta—non rimpiangerai questa decisione."* ("But I'm ready—you won't regret this decision.")

Olindo Parachini was a deeply kind man who was very sincerely interested in encouraging the development of young people. He saw the fire in my eyes, took a deep breath, and said, *"Va bene."* ("OK.")

And so, at the end of June of 1967, I was back at the Campeggio Inca. I was responsible for the well-being of seven girls, aged ten to thirteen or so, with all the various activities, and yes, I was in charge of the arts and crafts. This entailed trips to the hardware store in Olbia to buy putty, shellac, brushes, and paint for various projects; stockpiling empty tin cans from the kitchen; securing paper and drawing materials; and running the sessions.

In addition, this was 1967, and I had had acoustic guitar lessons. We sang Italian folk songs, and I had a repertoire of ten or eleven American folks songs that I could play—"If I Had a Hammer," "One Hundred Miles," "Blowin' in the Wind," and of course, "Kumbaya." One frequent post-siesta activity was to teach these songs to groups of campers and then perform them at the campfire gatherings. We assembled on a sand dune near the infirmary. I don't remember any mimeographed pages with printed lyrics. The campers learned the lyrics by my repeating them, of course, not entirely understanding what they were singing but singing very enthusiastically nonetheless. "Kumbaya, my Lord, Kumbaya!"

It was at the camp in 1967 that I met my first boyfriend. He was also working as a leader; we were the same age, sixteen. He was natively bilingual in French and Italian and spoke English fairly well. The relationship was almost exclusively in Italian, now taking my language skills in a new direction, towards the language of intimate relationships. In the summer of 1967 at the camp, the deal was sealed with a few chaste kisses.

We continued to see each other through the 1967–1968 academic year. My life that year was somewhat schizophrenic: I had my high school life at OSR during the week, of which he was almost not a part, and we spent parts of weekends together and talked endlessly on the phone at night. He was a student at a *liceo classico* in Rome, the high school focusing on humanities, as opposed to the *liceo scientifico*, for science. At the time, those two kinds of high school were the paths to a university education. His friends were native Romans, which had the simple consequence of deepening my knowledge of the Roman variety of Italian. I was now with my age mates, and I followed them linguistically quite willingly.

Ceil, YMCA leader, July 1968.

We returned to the camp as leaders in 1968 and in 1969. I graduated from OSR in June of 1968, at age seventeen. It was decided that I was too young to proceed to college in the United States—the choice that had been offered—so I stayed in Europe for the 1968–1969 academic year. So we were safe, at least until late August of 1969.

We returned to the camp in 1969 as part of the kitchen staff. This time, I had my own room in the area over the kitchen and shared a bathroom. Room and board came with the job. This was about cooking three meals a day for probably seventy campers and leaders—huge aluminum pots of pasta, enormous bowls of salad, tall paper bags of rolls delivered still warm to the camp every morning from the town baker, dark plum jam in round, ten-pound tins, huge vats of hot tea for the afternoon snack. And the washing of everything in two enormous sinks. No dishwasher in this kitchen yet. The water had to be hot enough to cut through the grease, so we protected our hands with yellow plastic gloves. And we sweated into the sinks, hair sticking to our necks. When the work was done, we had time until the next meal, so we swam and sat on the beach and read. It was new and liberating to not have responsibilities for campers and their activities. Behind the kitchen was the sandy bocce court. At 9 a.m., it was still in the shade. My favorite thing to do—and one of my most enduring memories—was to sit by myself on the edge of the bocce court after breakfast was done and sip a cup of coffee in the silent, cool shade, barefoot. Sometimes I smoked a cigarette, usually one of my father's Kents. I could count on about forty minutes of peace.

After camp that summer, we hitchhiked from Rome along the Calabrian coast, camping on beaches as we went and being fed lavishly by the truck drivers who picked us up. These truckers were natives of Calabria and Sicily, with only a theoretical awareness of standard Italian, be it written or spoken. They spoke to us in their dialects—really, separate languages—and we listened and learned.

In June of 1969, without any kind of conversation whatsoever, much less a lecture, my mother got me a prescription for birth control pills. "If you're going to have sex," she said, "take these, one a day, and don't miss any." We had been using the old withdraw-at-the-last-possible-second method and no doubt had some very close calls. It was the late 1960s, and we were seventeen. That was what we had figured out to do; it evidently didn't occur to us to ask anyone about these matters.

My oldest sister had gotten married at age nineteen while still in college. While she was not pregnant when she got married, there was the predictable baby ten months later, and my parents were not about to let me make what they perceived to be the same mistake. I don't know for sure, but they also probably didn't want me marrying a bilingual European. Their main concern was for me to have my twenties and get an education. My sister got the latter but not the former.

But the end of August 1969 came, and we played the departure scene at Fiumicino Airport on Friday, August 15, the day that Woodstock started in Upstate New York. My sister had come to escort me to Washington State, where I was to attend Whitman College in the town of Walla Walla, and we came through JFK Airport with terminals full of hippies from all over the United States. Young women were smoking marijuana in the restrooms. I stared without compunction, wide-eyed.

My boyfriend and I both wept copiously at the airport, but I held an excitement about this new adventure, which I didn't feel that I could openly admit to anyone: I had not lived in the United States since I was five years old and was deeply curious to see what life would be like there. I felt completely safe, thinking that I could come back to Italy for holidays and would eventually settle there. So, no sweat, let's go see how it is. I probably could have insisted and not left, but I wanted to go.

I first heard of Walla Walla and Whitman College in the fall of 1967. After a childhood outside the United States, I had been told, "Okay, you're going to college in the United States—no discussion— and we need to decide where." At the time, one of my sisters was with her family in Mt. Vernon, Washington, in the Skagit Valley, about an hour north of Seattle, and the other one was living in Seattle proper. But the University of Washington in Seattle had forty thousand students. I came from a graduating class of forty-nine, very small by American standards. I'm a strong swimmer, but I was afraid that I'd quickly drown in a school of that size.

Whitman is a small liberal arts college like Oberlin, Pomona, and Middlebury, with a student body in 1969 of about twelve hundred. Walla Walla is in the far southeast corner of the state, not far from the

Hanford nuclear production site. It was an eight-hour trip from Seattle by car, and it was right in the middle of miles of wheat and pea fields. It is named for Marcus and Narcissa Whitman, missionaries killed by the Cayuse Indians in the so-called Whitman massacres in 1847. Marcus, a Methodist minister whose earth-shattering motto, of which we were frequently reminded, was, "All my plans require time and distance."

Walla Walla is a classic American town with a main street and blocks of charming Victorian homes, the kind of town that can be found in Maryland, Indiana, Iowa, Kansas, Nebraska. It is also the site of the Washington State Penitentiary. There was and still is the familiar town vs. gown tension since the main activity of the area, other than the college, is farming. It has softened somewhat in the past forty years as wineries stretch across the valleys, attracting new income and new clientele.

But in August of 1969, Walla Walla was decidedly small-town America. Most of the Whitman students were from Washington State with a few from Idaho, Oregon, and California. And me, the zoo animal from Rome in Italy. There was a freshman look-book with all our photos and places of origin, and I felt as if some people sought me out just to peer at me and make sure that I didn't have a tail or horns. I can't say that I'd ever been to small-town America before August of 1969, and the first semester was a total blur, figuring out what was expected, how to be. I spoke English and of course understood everything being said to me, but I didn't always know how to behave. Dinner in a cafeteria at 5:30 p.m.? I was starving by nine! Sororities and the pressure to join one; I resisted.

Most days, I'd go straight from dinner to the library and stay there until nine, paralyzed with fear that I would flunk out if I didn't read every word assigned. When I got my first grade report in December and it said, "4.0, A in every course," I checked the envelope to make sure they had sent it to the right person. I decided that I could relax a bit for the spring semester. I did, but I never relaxed into drugs, as a number of friends did, some postponing their graduations and some never finishing. And, probably quite predictably, I gravitated to the most European thing I could find, the theatre department. There I found creative and funny people who felt comfortable with European things, though they did do American plays and musicals as well. There were a number of gay students in the theatre department. It was 1969, and the closet door was still firmly closed—but they too felt comfortable. Several of them later succumbed to AIDS because we didn't know yet.

I was in productions all through college, developed lifelong friendships, and to my parents' relief, found a husband. He was a theatre major, and the marriage lasted only eight years, but the hidden agenda—find a husband—had been fulfilled, so they accepted him. That was the expectation: the inscription in the cookbook given to us on our wedding day—one week after I graduated from Whitman—was "Congratulations on your MRS. Degree!"

I came to love Walla Walla. It turned out to be the perfect introduction to America, a very suitable door into the States. I still have friends there and have been back a number of times.

The boyfriend and I managed to keep the relationship going with phone calls and letters and holiday visits through July of 1971. We worked as leaders at the new YMCA site in Palena in the Abruzzo region in the summer of 1970. My parents moved back to the United States in June of 1971, at the end of my junior year at Whitman, and I found a junior-year abroad program in Rome for the 1971–1972 academic year, the plan being to live with my boyfriend, a plan approved by all four parents. And in July of 1971, as I was packing to fly back to Rome for that year, I received the Dear Jane letter: he had a new girlfriend, was living with her, and I should have no expectations that we would be together anymore. But I was committed to going, and I went. I walked through a scorching Rome the weekend of the Ferragosto holiday, August 14 and 15, when, in those days, the city completely emptied, as residents decamped to the beach or the mountains and stores remained closed in some cases for the whole month. I walked through the empty streets around Stazione Termini and the Basilica of Santa Maria Maggiore and contemplated my unexpected change of plans.

* * *

Olindo Parachini passed in his early nineties. He had long retired from the YMCA but had maintained a very active schedule as a translator of theological texts, working between English, French, German, and Italian. I kept in touch with him via email and by visiting him and his wife several times at their home north of Rome. He gave me my first real job and a large measure of confidence along with it.

The British Council

July and August afternoons in Rome are dry and hot, especially between 2 and 4 p.m. Flawless blue sky, cloudless, no hint of a breeze. Way too hot to be doing something outdoors, like hitting a tennis ball against the wall of the elementary school across from our house or riding a bike. Summer vacation, family trips already done. My best friend was at the beach on many of those afternoons, so there was no one to play with. There was a pool open to the public in EUR, one that had been built for the volleyball competitions during the Olympics. It was prohibitively expensive. I did get invited along to the beach often enough, but the key word was "invitation"; I couldn't really volunteer myself.

We didn't own a television until I was sixteen, and there wouldn't have been anything to watch during those hours anyway. During the 1960s, the two available channels provided English and math lessons for Italian adults at those times, no children's programs until about 5 p.m. When I did watch children's programs, it was with our Indian neighbors next door. The programs came on between 5 and 7 p.m.—*Stanlio e Olio* (*Laurel and Hardy*) in Italian, improbably spoken with American accents; *La Nonna del Corsaro Nero* (*The Grandmother of the Black Pirate*), a fantasy for children; some other dubbed American programs.

My parents finally relented and bought a TV during the fall of 1967 when an Italo-French production of the *Odyssey* was presented over eight weeks—stunning. Television finally allowed me access to the nightly grouping of commercials called *Carosello*, each commercial a mini-drama, the fabulous Saturday night variety show, *Studio Uno*, with the two impossibly tall and leggy German twins, *le Sorelle Kessler* with their famous *Dadaumpa* song, and the evening news, *Il Telegiornale della Sera*.

What there was to do was read. Our public library with books in English was the British Council, located in the tightly packed center of

Rome. On a day without too much traffic, the drive from our house in the south end of the city took about a half-hour. The library was located on the second floor with tens of beige metal, floor-to-ceiling shelves containing hundreds of books on all possible topics. The British Council has branches all over the world with the stated purpose of "promoting abroad a wider appreciation of British culture and civilization [by] encouraging cultural, educational and other interchanges between the United Kingdom and elsewhere." The Rome branch had opened in 1945, either during or right after World War II, creating a small island of British civility in a staggering and seriously bruised city. On special school excursions, we went there in the evenings to see Lawrence Olivier in the black-and-white films, *Hamlet* and *Othello*.

And I'd be taken there on summer days between 1961 and 1967 with my library card to gather a pile of books, enough to last for two weeks. I gravitated to fiction for teenagers—*Black Beauty* by Anna Sewell, *The Cricket in Times Square* by George Selden, *Little House on the Prairie* and its sibling volumes, and a number of books by Gerald Durrell—*My Family and Other Animals, A Zoo in My Luggage, The Drunken Forest.* His brother Lawrence Durrell was the well-known and sober novelist, author of *The Alexandria Quartet.* Gerald was a down-to-earth naturalist and zookeeper with a gift for hilarious prose about the antics of animals and humans. They were both born in India where their parents had also been born so, curiously, members of the colonial community but natives of India. Their father worked as an engineer.

I would take my pile of books home and make my way through them during those hot afternoons. I sat on the floor of my bedroom near the large window with filtered light coming through the horizontal blinds. I also read a weekly British newspaper for girls called *School Friend.* It featured four or five serial stories in comic form, along with games and puzzles. I don't know how my mother learned about it—no doubt from the parents of other girls my age. It arrived every week looking like a ten-inch pipe wrapped in brown paper. I waited with great anticipation to find out the latest developments in the continuing stories. And so I read, and so the afternoons passed.

I did get invited to go to the beach often enough. My friend's family were members of the beach establishment—*lo stabilimento balneare*—named Kursaal, situated in a long line of other such establishments on the beach of Ostia. From EUR, we could reach Ostia by car in under thirty minutes. Kursaal had been built in 1950 and had the usual rows of small cabins for changing. It had a fifty-meter salt-water pool marked with three-, five-, and ten-meter diving boards. I negotiated the three- and five-meter boards but never did get off the ten-meter one. I did stand on the edge of it several times but never had the courage to jump.

A trip to the beach meant bringing a full lunch to be consumed around 1 p.m.—plastic containers full of cold pasta, mixed salad, fruit salad, and of course, bread and wine, all consumed picnic-style near the changing cabin. Swimming was strictly forbidden for exactly one hour after lunch—"You will drown if you swim immediately after lunch!"— so we napped or played foosball, the soccer game in a waist-high box with plastic players attached to rotating rods. When we could swim, we alternated between the actual Mediterranean and the Kursaal pools, making up endless games that involved holding our breath under water while humming little tunes and acting out as many invented and bizarre scenes as we could—"Okay, now we're cleaning house! Now we're setting the table!"—before we had to come up for air. We didn't have masks so we couldn't actually see what the others were doing, of course.

A completely different beach experience involved going to the free beach in the area named Torvaianica, slightly south of Ostia. My parents had not seen a need to join a beach establishment like Kursaal when the free beach could be reached in thirty minutes. On beach evenings, my mother would prepare a picnic, and we would leave the house as soon as my father got home from work. We'd usually be there right after five thirty and had time for a swim and the picnic before sunset. The beach at that hour was usually deserted. No changing cabins or snack bar—we wore our suits under our clothes—just the beach and the empty dunes with their greyish sand and fading light.

The Opera at Caracalla

The construction of the Baths of Caracalla was begun in AD 206 by the emperor Settimio Severo and completed by his son Caracalla by AD 217. The baths cover sixty-two acres and were fed by water from one of the Roman aqueducts. These were public baths that remained in operation until the sixth century when the invading Goths damaged the aqueducts. One area lent itself to the construction of a huge performance space, and in 1937, the Teatro dell'Opera di Roma began to stage operas there during the summer months. The initial eight thousand seats became twenty thousand. Performances were suspended during World War II. They resumed in 1945 and continued uninterrupted until 1993, forty-eight years. After a period of renovation, they began again in 2001.

I was first taken to the opera at Caracalla in the summer of 1961. I was ten and the 8 p.m. curtain time was technically almost past my bedtime. The seating area was indeed enormous, rows upon rows of folding seats. A number of huge tour buses stood empty, their passengers making their way to the seats. These were the warm Roman summer nights, but we brought cardigans for the 1 a.m. final curtain. The first opera was Verdi's *Aida,* an enormous production with, as the Friday July 7 review in the *Paese Sera* newspaper stated, *"animali di ogni genere"* (animals of all types). In his book *Great Opera Disasters*, Hugh Vickers recounts Peter Ustinov's experience with his young daughter at a Caracalla performance of *Aida* during the same 1961 summer when "camels, elephants, horses, unwanted cats etc. . . . . all relieved themselves simultaneously. As he stared aghast at this incredible sight, he felt a light tapping on his shoulder, and his daughter's earnest voice—'Daddy, is it all right if I laugh?'" I can't say that I remember camels or elephants, but I clearly remember horses straining, eyes wide, against the shock of the huge, applauding audience and the very loud orchestra just below them. There were at least two intermissions during which vendors roamed through the audience crying, *"Birracocacaffè !"* all one word for beer, coke, and coffee.

And there was of course the music and the staging—the intensity of the full orchestra, the rousing triumphal march, the lovely "Celeste Aida" sung by Radames, the wrenching duet "Addio, terra" sung in the tomb in which Aida and Radames would perish, the excellent illusion of the Nile created by undulating blue fabric and lighting, the contrast between the tiny figures of Aida and Radames in the cavernous tomb. I was totally taken by the idea that they were willing to suffocate for love and wondered how long that would actually take.

Aida was followed by productions of *Madama Butterfly*, *Tosca*, *Rigoletto*, *Otello*, *La Bohème*, and *Il Trovatore* over the course of the next three or four summers. During the 1967–1968 academic year, our senior year at OSR, the parents of about five of us went together on a box for the opera season at the downtown opera house located near the central station. We dressed appropriately on Sunday evenings, traveled by metro, and generally behaved well in the box. The productions—*Cenerentola* by Rossini, *Egmont* by Beethoven, *Lulu* by Berg, *The Rake's Progress* by Stravinsky—were part of a whole different genre of opera not that well suited for the outdoors and more general audiences, but they certainly broadened our exposure.

Italian opera has continued to be one soundtrack of my adult life from Monteverdi through Puccini. I am taken by arias—"E Lucevan le Stelle" in *Tosca*, Musetta's "Quando M'en Vo" in *La Bohème*, "Casta Diva" in *Norma*—and by the astonishing harmonies when quartets and quintets of singers are allowed to just stand and sing, as in the end of act 2 and act 3 in *La Bohème*. I am invariably moved to tears by "Va' Pensiero" from *Nabucco*, the de facto Italian national anthem. And as a sociolinguist, I am taken by the role that operas and their librettos, written in standard Italian, played in the unification of the country alongside compulsory elementary school education—*la scuola dell'obbligo*—and newspapers and magazines published in standard Italian. An overall fascination that started on a warm Roman night in 1961.

The Flood of 1966

The Arno River flows from the Apennine Mountains through Florence to the Mediterranean Sea near Pisa. The end of October and the beginning of November of 1966 saw very unusual amounts of rainfall, threatening dams upstream on November 3. On November 4, engineers feared that the Valdarno dam would burst and discharge water that would reach Florence at a speed of thirty-seven miles per hour. Generators failed, landslides obstructed roads, and all of Florence was flooded, up to twenty-two feet in the Santa Croce area. A number of markers were installed on walls around the city to show how high the water had risen. The contents of the jewelry and gold shops on the Ponte Vecchio were thoroughly emptied out into the riverbed. One hundred one people were killed, and millions of books and masterpieces of art were damaged or destroyed. Whole basements filled with priceless manuscripts filled up with stinking muddy water. Once the rain stopped, Ponte Vecchio merchants tramped through the muddy riverbed hoping to retrieve at least some of their wares, and books and works of art began to be taken to areas where they could be tended to.

On that weekend, my parents and I had traveled to Saturnia, a thermal spa located in southern Tuscany, due south of Florence. Saturnia has been known since the time of the Etruscans; its facilities have greatly expanded, and it is now a very popular destination. It was not as well frequented in early November of 1966, and we were the only clients in the hotel on the site. Bathing in the thermal pool, in which large clumps of sulphurous moss floated, and sitting under the waterfall located at one end of the pool were punctuated by excellent Tuscan meals and reading. No television in hotel rooms in those days. I was fifteen, a high school junior, and battling my way through *The American* by Henry James. A school assignment. I remember it precisely because it was such a dense read; I was too young for it, and I have never gone back to it.

Since there was no television and we didn't have access to a news-paper that weekend, we had no clear picture of what had happened. We had driven to Saturnia up the coast highway with no incident. We were in Tuscany but clueless. We did find out when we arrived home on Sunday to see television news and the Sunday *Daily American* with its ghastly black-and-white images of the flood. And not too long after the weekend of the flood, some of my classmates and I were summoned to a conference facility in our area of the city, EUR. The organizers had no doubt contacted various schools including ours. In several enormous rooms, books that had been rescued from the flooded Florence base-ments had been laid out on long waist-high rows of wooden tables. The books of all sizes were still soaking wet. We were each given an apron, a plastic card the size of a credit card, and a stack of thick paper towels—*carta assorbente*—the same paper that we found in our school notebooks for absorbing the ink of our fountain pens. Our task was to work on one book at a time, to very gently separate the pages with the plastic card and to place a piece of paper towel between them, and then do it again until we got to the end of the book and moved on to a new one. We chatted and separated pages and chatted during several sessions lasting seven or eight hours. We were technically not among *gli angeli del fango* (the angels of the mud), hundreds of volunteers who descended on Florence to participate in this rescue process (and so won-derfully depicted in the 2003 film *La meglio gioventù*), but we did our small part. The whole room had a very pungent and persistent smell of muddy water, and to this day, whenever I smell wet paper—not actually that often, I must say—I am immediately transported to the room with the soaked books.

Sunday Dinner

Our weekday dinners in Italy were unmistakably American: meat, potatoes, some kind of vegetable, sometimes cornbread and pinto beans, sometimes a salad instead of the vegetable, all on one plate. It was served at 7:30 p.m., after my father's nap and his cocktail with my mother. That's what my New Mexico–raised father insisted on. My mother was a trained dietician, so I'm pretty sure that I never ate an unbalanced meal until I encountered the dinner buffet at Whitman College.

On Sundays, we would venture out into the hinterlands of Rome, in the province of Lazio, to find a trattoria for lunch. We were invariably in the company of many other Romans. The best places were the ones with four or five tables and no written menu. We were almost always the first customers to arrive, so the tablecloths were still slightly damp and warm from the laundry. In the summer and fall, we would sit outside, but in the winter and early spring, these places were dark inside, with a little chill around the edges. What was to be eaten was negotiated with the waiter, who was probably also the proprietor. And the best dish was the simplest: spaghetti with a red sauce, with meat or without, a small amount of parmesan cheese on top. The spaghetti was always perfectly al dente. The fork was accompanied by a large spoon, truck-driver style.

Over fifty years later, it is almost impossible for me to order anything else in Italy or Italian restaurants here. I very carefully read and study the menu and then order spaghetti with red sauce. Every time. I am constantly trying to recapture that flavor from the 1960s, either at home or eating out. My friends tease me for always ordering the same thing, jokingly suggesting that maybe we should call the restaurant beforehand to make sure that they haven't run out of the basic ingredients: "Are you sure that we shouldn't call Dino's to make sure, in Italy, he has enough tomato sauce?" I laugh and order spaghetti with red sauce.

Church, Part II

Not long after we arrived in Rome, my mother became aware of the Episcopal church in downtown Rome—St. Paul's Inside the Walls, in contrast to the papal Basilica of Saint Paul Outside the Walls, founded by the emperor Constantine and expanded under Valentinian in the AD 370s. The Episcopal one was completed in 1880 in a Gothic revival style, the first Protestant church to be built in Rome, just ten years after the unification of Italy. It is a church of the Convocation of Episcopal Churches in Europe.

St. Paul's Within the Walls, Rome.

St. Paul's Within the Walls on Via Nazionale, Rome.

The church was on Via Nazionale, a major thoroughfare in downtown Rome, and we lived in the south end of the city, so getting there in time for the 11 a.m. service on Sundays and finding a parking spot was a focused project.

My father exhibited the same ambivalence about church-going that we had seen in Guatemala and often opted out, but I was pressed into joining my mother on the Sundays that we were in town, from the fall of 1960 through the end of April 1966—almost six years. It, of course, involved being washed, coiffed, and dressed up and sitting politely in the hard wooden pew, singing hymns at the appropriate intervals. There was reading material in the form of the New Testament, several copies in the rack on the back of each pew, so I often distracted myself with that. There was the inevitable sermon and announcements from the pulpit. And once again, as at the Union Church, my attention was drawn to the extraneous—the church was fairly dark inside, even at midday, with the stained glass windows providing most of the illumination, and I studied every inch of them; there are always candles, and the solemn procession-al and recessional walks down the aisle by the minister and the choir, singing and dressed in colorful robes.

As in Guatemala, I never paid much attention to the message being sent down from the pulpit, but I was suddenly forced to deal with it directly in the spring of 1966, as I was enrolled in the catechism classes that would lead to my confirmation in the church. There were six other young people in the catechism classes, which met after school once a week for six weeks in a meeting room at the church. We went over reli-gious materials and prepared to answer specific questions that would be put to us during the confirmation ceremony.

I was completely outraged about the whole thing because the six-week commitment meant that I would not be able to partici-pate in the spring musical production at school; I could not miss one whole after-school rehearsal per week leading up to the performances. Confirmation had been decided for me; I had no interest at all in being confirmed, but at fifteen, I could not object very effectively. I was going to do this, period.

And so it was on Sunday, April 24, 1966, with the Right Reverend Stephen F. Bayne Jr. in charge, I was confirmed in the Episcopal Church.

Confirmation card, Episcopal Church.

I answered my assigned questions; a reception followed the service. And that marked the formal end of my career as any kind of churchgoer. I have not entered a church except as a guest at a wedding, baptism, or funeral or as student of art history since that day. My abiding suspicion and misgivings that I had consistently missed the point of church— suspicion and misgivings that started to make themselves known at the Union Church in Guatemala—finally came around to the very front of my brain and were clearly there to stay.

So my confirmation was definitely accomplished—as a lifelong non-churchgoer—not the confirmation the adults had imagined, much to their very obvious chagrin.

St. Paul's Within the Walls provided a space in the basement for the Teen Club, a Saturday night dance party for American teens and their friends. Sometimes the music was provided by a live band. I was allowed to go starting at age thirteen, delivered to the spot by someone's parents, sometimes mine. Teen Club is the source of some stark adolescent memories. I was the classic wallflower: I was always a head shorter than all my classmates; I wore pointy glasses, and my hair was awkwardly styled. I had nice legs and a cute butt, but my chest was as flat as a smooth pine board. I was quite decidedly not one of the popular kids. I stood against the basement wall, waiting for someone to ask me to dance. No one did, ever. But I kept going, never sharing my misery with my parents.

I've been tempted to go back to that basement to look for the curved indentation that my backside must have forged in the brick wall as I stood waiting. There may be a similar indentation in the wall in the OSR cafeteria where school dances were held. Things started to look up after I met my boyfriend in the summer of 1967 and dispensed with Teen Club and school dances.

1530/Home Leave

In even-numbered years, starting in 1958, my parents and I came back to the United States on home leave. This was built into the service of many Americans working overseas. The usual destination for us was our house in Phoenix. We always called it "1530." It was 1530 W. Glenrosa, Phoenix, Arizona, in a quiet but distinct neighborhood of North Phoenix, not far from the downtown area.

The house was built in 1948, four years after my parents moved from Colorado to Phoenix. I was born in March of 1951, and it was my first home until we moved to Guatemala City in August of 1956. We owned it for forty-one years, until the spring of 1989, when my mother sold it and moved to Washington State to live closer to my oldest sister.

The house had three bedrooms, a combination living room/dining room and a decent-sized kitchen. The kitchen window looked out on a large backyard with a clothesline and the canal, built by the Salt River Project to provide water to this thirsty city. Our canal, one of eight, was the Grand Canal, the oldest remaining pioneer canal on the north side of the Salt River. It was planned in 1877 and constructed in 1878 by the Grand Canal Company. The federal government purchased the Grand Canal for $20,488 in June 1906. At that time, the canal served about seventeen thousand acres.

All the fifteen or so houses on our block were identical in layout. The rules about small children walking unaccompanied along the canal were very strict, not to be challenged. This was the Phoenix of dry heat, easily 104 degrees at noon during the hottest months, so hot that the sidewalks did not cool off at night. One could hear the neighbors sitting on their porches until very late at night, chatting, or as we called it, "visiting."

The Lucas residence, 1530 W. Glenrosa, Phoenix, in 1958.

Once a month during the hottest months, my father would get up at 4 a.m. and go into the backyard to lift a small metal gate that allowed water from the canal to flood the backyard and the front lawn to give Phoenicians the illusion that they lived in the Midwest where green lawns are plausible.

Fairly early I acquired a vocabulary of the names of trees, bushes, and other plants since the front yard had a date palm, a pecan tree, a weeping willow, which succumbed to the blades of a push lawn mower, two pyracantha bushes on either side of the front window, and a flower garden in front of the porch.

The sidewalks had smooth edges, and in the cement walkway leading from the front door, there are still the three small handprints of my two sisters and me.

The walkway at 1530 W. Glenrosa, Phoenix, summer of 1951.

The pervasive hot weather called for a large inflatable swimming pool in the backyard with the picnic table bench serving as a slide into the water. We made grape Kool-Aid popsicles in an ice tray and sucked on them while holding them in paper towels and ran through the tepid fountains made by holding one's thumb over the opening of the plastic garden hose. When we wanted a real pool, we walked west along the canal to Nelson's Pool, the community pool at which all were welcome for a small fee. It was always full on weekend afternoons—young 1950s Phoenicians laughing and squealing with truck-sized inner tubes; the chlorine coming off the bright turquoise water fairly shimmered.

The backyard also had fruit trees planted by my mother—orange, grapefruit, and apricot. I was still learning, before age five, the difference between appropriate responses and mouthing off, so more than once I was sent to the apricot tree. "Go out and select a switch," my mother would say sternly. The switch was specifically for mouthing off, as opposed to a swat on my backside for non-verbal bad behavior. I would very slowly walk out and select the shortest and most slender apricot branch I could find, weeping as I went. She would wait for me at the kitchen door and swiftly apply it to my calves when I handed it to her. It stung for sure, but as she well knew, the worst part of the punishment was the humiliation of the walk to the tree and having to select my own instrument of punishment.

This was the only place that all five of us—father, mother, two sisters, and I—lived together for three continuous years. My sisters were twelve and fourteen when I was born, so when my parents and I moved to Guatemala City in 1956, the younger sister, Ellen Adona, known as Doni, stayed in Phoenix to finish high School, and the elder, Jane, got married. Our move to Guatemala was magical, but it broke the spell of 1530.

Jane (*left*), Doni (*right*), and Ceil (*center*) Lucas, Easter 1955.

So, home leave. This was when I first watched American TV and learned about current American culture in two- to three-week doses. A handful of episodes each time of *Lassie*, *The Mickey Mouse Club*, Disney's *Fantasyland*, and my parents' favorite, *The Lawrence Welk Show*. On some oppressive Phoenix afternoons, I would sit in the darkened living room with my grandmother Jane, known as Mommy B (for her last name, Bradley) as she watched her stories—*As the World Turns*, *Search for Tomorrow*—or a movie in a showcase matinee. She sat riveted.

Home leave for my mother meant absolutely essential shopping for me at J. C. Penney or Sears, mostly for underwear and, inevitably, a new pair of saddle shoes, either brown and white or black and white, with socks to go with them. I wore them through the four years in Guatemala, but by early 1960 in Rome, it began to be clear to my mother that we were living in one of the finest and most creative locations for the production of shoes on earth—Italy—and that the Italians could be trusted to make shoes that would be healthy for young feet. That meant, mercifully, no more saddle shoes.

On two occasions, home leave included being enrolled for two weeks in a Phoenix-area school. One of these was the Encanto Elementary School, about six blocks from our house. It is still there. The two weeks in an American school were a confusing blur. The teachers wanted to be called by their last names, with Mrs. or Miss. Everything was in English, of course. And there was the matter of standing and facing the American flag at the beginning of the day to recite something called the Pledge of Allegiance. No one bothered to show me a printed copy of it or explain what the purpose of this might be. I had the good sense to stand, but I never did learn the pledge in its entirety.

There was recess in the already-hot morning sun and lunch in the cafeteria, during which we were each given a tray and asked to choose what we wanted from the serving pans attended by older ladies wearing hairnets. I was completely taken by the milk served in cardboard pints and by the water fountains that we called "bubblers."

My mother had noticed that the United Nations would pay for any form of home leave travel, round trip. She said, "Why fly when they will pay for us to go by boat?" So our home leave travel involved four separate trips on ocean liners. We always had second-class accommodations, perfectly comfortable but a distinction that mattered to some.

The Holland America Line (courtesy of the Hoboken Historical Museum).

Ocean liner's arrival in New York, 1966.

When we moved to Rome in 1960, we took the *Flandre*, built in 1951 and operated by the French Line. On this trip, we were invited to dinner at the captain's table and dined with a very lively and entertaining Peter Ustinov. Dinner, of course, always required dressing up and was accompanied by daily printed cardboard menus. We sailed from New York to Le Havre and toured Paris. We later took the USS *Independence*, run by the American Export Lines. It made stops in the Canary Islands and Casablanca, where we roamed through the city and the souk for a day.

A trip on the Holland Line's *Rotterdam* brought us to Amsterdam and Delft, and a trip on the Cunard Line's *Queen Mary* got us to London and Stratford-upon-Avon. We experienced the iconic arrival in New York Harbor with the Statue of Liberty and the Empire State Building. I can't say that I knew it was an iconic view at the time, just the end of another crossing.

Bert, Ceil, and Kathleen Lucas, arrival in New York Harbor, 1966.

I don't remember there ever being very many kids my age on these seven-day crossings. The few of us that there were roamed endlessly around the boats, exploring every corner. Each liner had a swimming pool, but the salt water sloshed fiercely and was cold in the North Atlantic air. There was always a movie theatre, and to pass the time, we went to several showings of the same movie, eventually reciting the dialogue along with the actors. My bad adolescent habit of chewing my fingernails was permanently halted during one such showing: I was munching away when the older European gentleman sitting next to me simply reached over and gently moved my hand from my mouth to my lap, never saying a word. That ended a years-long habit. I never saw him after the showing.

The most remarkable thing about these trips is that they are almost no longer possible. A September 2015 piece in the *Washington Post* tells of the recent sailing of the *Queen Mary II*, but by the end of the 1960s, with the rapid advent of transatlantic air travel, ocean crossings came to be seen as quaint and inefficient. Many of the liners were re-purposed as cruise ships, and the *Queen Mary* now serves as a floating hotel in Long Beach, California. My mother's instinct had let us be part of the end of the era of ocean liners that had started in the mid-nineteenth century.

Home leave meant being around my sisters for several weeks. We had lived together as a family for three years, between March of 1951, when I was born, and August of 1954, when Jane went off to Northern Arizona University in Flagstaff.

Starting in August of 1956, the next sixteen years of my life were spent in Guatemala, Rome, and college in Washington State. Until 1969, I saw Jane and Doni only every two years. My parents of course kept in touch with them, and I heard a lot about their lives. Doni made a short visit to Guatemala and lived in Rome for almost a year between 1960 and 1961; Jane never came to Guatemala and came to Italy only in 1969 to escort me back to college. She had married in 1956 and, by 1964, had three children. She had a gift of understanding very small children and voluntarily ran a nursery school in her home for many years. She was also a skilled watercolor painter, painting the landscapes of Washington State with their pines and alders and old barns. If she could have fed herself books with a big spoon, she would have, mostly historical fiction. She was mostly of my mother's side with her dark hair, but her green eyes may have come from Al Lucas, her paternal grandfather.

Doni became a registered nurse, worked in many hospitals, and did some private duty nursing in Rome. She was very much of her paternal grandmother's side with red hair and a freckled complexion. Both were creatures of the western United States: Jane had been born in Ganado, Arizona, in the Presbyterian hospital located in the Navajo Nation where my mother had worked. Doni was born in Fort Defiance and raised in Phoenix, so she was also an Arizona native. She lived some years in Seattle and Kalamazoo, Michigan, but always came home. She was married once, very late by the standards of her generation, and very unhappily. We saw each other more frequently as adults, but the pattern of one or two visits a year had been set very early; never any long stays. They were more like aunts than sisters to me.

They are both gone now, Doni in 1989 and Jane in 2014. For siblings, our lives were lived very far apart and very differently.

Getting Finished

The school year in Guatemala ran from January to the end of November with December off, so when we left in May of 1960, I was in the middle of fourth grade. When we got to Rome, my parents and the teachers decided to give me a shot directly at fifth grade in the fall of 1960. It worked out, but the long-term result was that when I graduated from high school in June of 1968, I was only seventeen. My fantasies of making a life in Italy and Europe did not match those of my parents at all, especially what my father envisioned for me. He was not at all interested in my half-Italian, half-Belgian boyfriend. And at seventeen, I was deemed not old enough to go off to college in America. It was 1968. "Dr. King Fatally Shot by Assassin in Memphis," the *New York Times* screamed on April 5. "Kennedy Shot!" cried the *Los Angeles Times* on June 6. On August 28, troops confronted anti-war demonstrators at the Democratic Convention in Chicago, demonstrators who had been gearing up since 1967. I had already been accepted to Whitman College at this point, but I suspect that my father saw what was going in the United States at that time, looked at me, and said, "No, she's not ready." I suspect he was worried that, given my demonstrated penchant for blending in, I would do just that and get involved in some kind of unruly student movement.

Not that Italy in the late 1960s and the 1970s was any kind of picnic. Those years have come be known as the *Anni di Piombo* (Years of Lead) because of the volume of shootings and violence, starting with student uprisings in 1968, continuing with the bombing of Piazza Fontana in Milan in December of 1969 (seventeen dead, eighty-eight wounded), and culminating with the assassination of the former prime minister, Aldo Moro, in 1978. The Red Brigades, a terrorist organization, claimed responsibility for Moro's death; responsibility for Piazza Fontana has never been determined. It is ironic that my father might have been concerned about what was going on in the United States while bombs were exploding around us.

So it had to be decided what I would do for the 1968–1969 academic year, besides spending time with the boyfriend when he was not in school. He still had a year to go at the Liceo Classico Augusta. We did, however, manage to play hooky on a number of occasions.

My mother had educated herself about Swiss finishing schools for girls and identified one, Pensionnat Riante-Rive (Smiling Shore) located in Lausanne on Lake Geneva. "Pensionnat" indicated that it provided room and board. Lausanne is known for its astonishing, dark forest, the Bois de Sauvelin.

Swiss finishing schools had always been popular for the education of girls in their late teens at a time when public education was not easily available to them, particularly girls from well-to-do families. They were especially popular in the years following the Second World War as an escape from the chaos enveloping Europe. It was decided that Riante-Rive would be a good place for me to spend the fall of 1968.

Pensionnat Riante-Rive brochure.

It had been founded in 1896 by Mademoiselle A. J. Capt. Her niece, Mademoiselle J. M. Thiébaud, had been the principal until her retirement, at which point she had handed the reins to her long-time collaborator, Mademoiselle H. Béné. Mademoiselle Béné was the principal during my four-month stay at the school, a short and stout woman with short reddish hair. A woman who, after just six years, had just about had enough of teenage girls in a rapidly changing world.

French—which included vocabulary, grammar, dictation, essays, literature, history of art and music, and Swiss geography—was compulsory. Optional subjects included other languages—English, German, Italian, Spanish—commercial correspondence and typing, music and art lessons, and various sports, such as riding, tennis, swimming, skating, and skiing. As for typing, this is 1968, still a long twenty-two years away from the personal computer and still considered a necessary skill for the well-educated young woman.

Most interesting was the optional area of domestic science: cooking, sewing, laundry, and ironing. The students in the fall of 1968 came from Venezuela, Peru, England, and Sweden. I was the only American. Except for Lisbet, the girl from Sweden, who became my good buddy, these girls came from very wealthy families, the British girl being a member of royalty.

In a 2011 article about one of the last surviving Swiss finishing schools, William Lee Adams observes, "Back home, four of the five women serving have live-in staffs. But the program requires them to rotate through the service role anyway so they can better train and manage their employees." Precisely.

The young women in my cohort were not learning how to make beds properly or how to operate a vacuum so they could then perform these tasks themselves. No, no. They were learning so they could then supervise their household workers. Lisbet and I came from decidedly more modest situations and knew damn well that we wouldn't be having to teach someone to run the vacuum or dust. The realization of why these young women were being taught domestic science made me chuckle even then.

Ceil in Lausanne, October 1968.

Meals of course were quite formal, and we were reminded of the proper way to eat bread and jam at breakfast—one is to break a small piece off the slice of bread and apply butter and jam to it; one is not supposed to apply butter and jam to the whole slice and bite down on it all of a piece, which Lisbet and I did quite regularly. We sat across from each other at the end of the long table and were delighted when we were served mashed potatoes. We would proceed to load up the backs of our forks as high as we could—mashed potatoes as the binding agent for peas, meat—and send it all into our mouths at once, trying to not laugh out loud and to avoid the withering gaze of Mlle. Béné. She never caught us.

I took advantage of other course offerings and started to learn how to read non-fiction without being told to. I started getting up an hour before breakfast to sit alone on the back porch with a cup of instant coffee to read—mostly the history of theatre for the next phase that was coming in January of 1969. I had a one-on-one German lesson once a week in town, requiring me to ride the public bus. We were exposed to horseback riding and ice skating, revealing at a fairly early age my complete ineptitude for both, saving me a lot of time in later life. In the case of horseback riding, I was assigned to a horse which rapidly sensed my discomfort and took off running with me on him; I narrowly avoided decapitation as he ran under a low and sturdy tree branch; as for ice skating, as much as I wanted to learn because it looked so pretty on TV, I simply never got the hang of it and, with burning ankles, could not wait to get the skates off.

But the enormous advantage of the four months at Riante-Rive was that French was required. Period. The school brochure states, in bold: "A rule, strictly observed at all times, requires the pupils to speak nothing but French." And "at all times" meant exactly that: with Mlle. Béné, with the staff, with each other, during all waking hours. The moment of truth came every evening at dinner when we had to sign our names in *le carnet*—the notebook—confirming that we had spoken only French over the past twenty-four hours. To sign when one had spoken language other than French was highly dishonorable and could be challenged by Mlle. Béné or one of the staff who might have heard us. So, in addition to our daily French classes, we spoke French solidly for four months, and I made great strides with the language. I had started at age five at Evelyn's school in Guatemala ("in this world, you're gonna need languages") and continued through high school in Rome, won some kind of prize at graduation for French language skills, and these four months in Lausanne firmed everything up very solidly. I never had to lie in the notebook. The German didn't stick as well, and I eventually left it behind, but the French was there for good. I also attended a course on the history of French at the University of Lausanne, which let me see how a European university classroom worked.

I went on to become a French and art history major at Whitman in the fall of 1969, got a master's degree in French and Italian at the University of Texas, Austin, and a PhD in linguistics at Georgetown University. I ended up with a forty-year career as a professor of sign language linguistics at Gallaudet University in Washington, DC, and a teacher of Italian and French. A substantial part of the foundation of that career was built in Lausanne.

I'm entirely certain that I did not get finished in the way that was intended. I suspect that my mother dearly hoped that the school would get my attention about the niceties of social comportment and smooth over my somewhat rough edges—I was a demonstrated tomboy with a very direct manner. She was hoping for something more ladylike. I missed that part almost completely but came away with very strong French skills. I also suspect that, by then, she could also clearly see that I was fundamentally a creature of language and that's where I was headed personally and professionally. She came to graciously accept that fluent written and spoken French were worth a lot more than knowing how to teach the servants to vacuum or how to supervise the kitchen in the big house. She became even more accepting when languages ended up paying my mortgage and car insurance. "I'm going to be a dialect geographer!" I announced in our Rome kitchen one afternoon when I was about sixteen, not really knowing entirely yet what that entailed. She gave me a vague smile and continued to stir the potatoes, but she had a clue of where I was headed. As it turns out, I pretty much hit the mark.

The semester in Lausanne ended in December of 1968. I had expressed an interest at some point in costume design for the theatre, had done a bit of it for high school productions, so my mother somehow arranged for me to attend in the spring of 1969 the Pucci school of fashion design located in a building right on Piazza Navona. Never mind that I could not sew, had no interest in learning, and carry comical memories of the summer of 1965 when I was fourteen and my mother decided it was time for me to learn. She of course was a natural seamstress who could sew almost without a pattern, just envisioning the garment in her head and assembling it. I had almost no store-bought clothes except for jeans and coats until I went to college. She made everything—skirts, shirts, dresses, shorts with matching tops—and clearly felt that a well-raised girl should know how to sew. For her, an electric sewing machine was an essential possession. And she enjoyed it, got a real sense of accomplishment from completing a garment. The whole thing thoroughly frustrated me with the detail work and the pins, and I did not enjoy it one bit and longed to be reading my book. She got so frustrated one afternoon that she began to flail at my shoulder with a piece of folded fabric. I started to cry until we both started laughing at the absurdity of the whole thing. So that was the end of the sewing lessons, but off I went to Pucci.

I loved reading the history of theatre as it pertained to costume design from the Greeks to modern times and had started this reading in Lausanne the previous fall. Being the only non-Italian at Pucci, I was immersed in Italian every day and made great strides. But I started to re-alize that this might not be for me when we were required to design fab-ric for umbrellas—which bored me silly—and a poster for an important exhibition of Italian shoes. I had what I thought was the brilliant idea of having the god Mercury prominently featured on the poster—the winged god with a focus on his feet. The teacher was appalled: "Mercury is known as the patron of thieves!" a message that could not be sent with the poster.

A career in fashion or costume design was not to be. I finished up the semester at Pucci and began to focus on an August journey to Whitman College in Walla Walla, Washington. The enormous irony of this, of course, is that I was named for the American fashion designer Ceil Chapman (née Mitchell, 1912–1979) , born and raised on Staten Island. She worked in Manhattan, designing clothing for the likes of Elizabeth Taylor, Deborah Kerr, Greer Garson, Grace Kelly, Aretha Franklin, and other celebrities. And she saved me from the name my mother had in store for me. The deal was that, if I were a boy, I would be named William Albertrand Jr.; if I were a girl, it was my father's respon-sibility to find a name for me. I was already three days old and nameless when he spotted an ad in the Phoenix paper, the *Arizona Republic,* for Ceil Chapman fashions and said, "That'll do just fine." My mother, being my mother, had a backup in case he didn't come through, Debbie Beth, a good 1950s name for a white girl. I am eternally grateful to my father and Ceil Chapman.

Leaving

I always say that I spent twelve years in Rome because my unanticipated move back came in August of 1972. I was preparing to leave Italy to go back to Walla Walla for my senior year at Whitman College. I had spent the 1971–1972 academic year in Rome, my junior year. In December of 1970, after eleven years in Italy, my parents announced they were moving back to the States, specifically to Washington, DC, for my father's last job before retirement. I quickly informed them that I was in no way ready to leave Italy permanently. I had been in the States at college since the fall of 1969 but always came home for summers and Christmas—and, as I have mentioned, I set about finding a junior year abroad program. It ended up being through Temple University. It could have been through the University of Central Mars for all I cared—it just had to be in Rome with credits transferable to my home school.

When the school year was over, I then worked for seven weeks as a chambermaid at a beach hotel in Sperlonga—halfway between Rome and Naples. I cleaned rooms and did laundry and, once again, strongly reinforced my spoken Italian. My American boyfriend worked at the same hotel as a handyman. The owner of the hotel and our boss was an Italian woman in her early thirties. She knew that we would be there for only part of the summer. We took our meals in the kitchen and slept in an en-suite room off the kitchen. We read and went to the beach during our free time. He was slogging his way through *Middlemarch*, a formidable edition that had pages like tissue paper. As far as I remember, the payment was off the books, cash along with room and board. This was a beach hotel, so the bathtubs, sheets, and ceramic floors always had sand everywhere, sand that had to be removed. The hotel owned a washing machine but no dryer, so I carried the wet linens to the roof every day in a big plastic tub.

On August 24, 1972, I am sitting cross-legged on the roof of the hotel, where I hung the laundry, watching the sun set over the Mediterranean, alone. I am twenty-one years old. This departure from Italy is different. Yes, we had gone back to the United States every two years since 1956 on home leave, and I had left Italy in August of 1969 to go to college. But Italy and Rome were home, and I had always come home. But even though I had hoped I could complete college in the United States and then come back and get on with my life in Italy, I knew this plan had changed. My parents had left, as had most of my high school friends. The Italian boyfriend was out of the picture before I even arrived in August of 1971. I was going to graduate in December of 1972 and had no idea what I would do after that. But somehow I knew I would not be coming back to Italy to start a professional life there.

So I'm watching the sunset and trying to absorb what is about to happen. We left the United States in 1956 when I was five, and now I am about to move back. But leaving had never before felt like moving back.

AMERICA

Back to where I started: when I say, upon meeting someone new, "I wasn't raised here," "here" means America, the States—*gli States*, as many Italians call them, with the Italian definite article—and I think I mean that I can't be expected to know all things American or to always act like an American, although I'm not entirely sure what "act like an American" means.

Our parents and school administrators did manage to build an idea of America in us. Prom, yearbooks, cheerleaders and basketball tournaments with other American schools, Brownie Scouts and Girl Scouts, Halloween outings, Thanksgiving, American musicals, those things didn't just happen. Having now been at various times in administrative positions in a university, I know that each of the school-related things requires a specific decision because they require money and scheduling. Hard to tell who pushed harder, the American parents who wanted to maintain some piece of American identity in their children—parents who, for the most part, had been born and raised in the United States and came to Guatemala and Italy as adults and had every intention of someday resuming their lives in the United States or school administrators, many of them also born and raised in the United States and who wanted to keep the American part of an international education. No doubt it was some of both. They all chose which parts they thought were important. Home leave also helped build an awareness of American culture, but a strange, only every-two-years awareness.

What also strikes me are the parts of America that got left out in the presentations of the parents and school administrators, on purpose or not. For example, Rosa Parks had staged her protest on December 1, 1955, when I was four, and the major events in the Civil Rights movement proceeded to unfold: Little Rock in 1957; the 1963 March on Washington; the murder of Medgar Evers in 1963; the murders of

Michael Schwerner, James Chaney, and Andrew Goodman during the Freedom Summer of 1964; the Democratic Convention in Chicago in 1968; all events and circumstances that were at best vague to me when they happened. We had no English newspaper in Guatemala. In Rome, the *Daily American* summarized the news from the States pretty well. But the medium that deftly unified the youth of my generation, American television, was completely unavailable. Americans who have known me for a long time have stopped saying, "You probably never saw that show . . . " As I mentioned earlier, the murders of Martin Luther King and Bobby Kennedy in the spring and early summer of 1968 are very clear memories, which include the powerful reactions of faculty and staff born and raised in the United States. It was all very close for them. Likewise the war in Vietnam and American reactions to that.

I started catching up when I went to college in 1969, and since I have lived full-time in the United States starting in 1972, I have hungrily consumed the history of both the Civil Rights movement and the Vietnam War, in particular documentaries, always feeling slightly behind, "Wow! That was going on?" Not having been raised in America, I had to learn what it meant to be white. Not that either Guatemala or Italy was a nicely balanced multicultural society; certainly neither was. But I had not lived in a society with whites, blacks, Hispanics, Asians, all together. The only black people I had ever seen had been in Guatemala and spoke Spanish. During a trip to the grocery store in Phoenix in 1958, at age seven, I met a black man who was bagging the groceries. I immediately began chattering in Spanish to him. He gave me a gentle, quizzical look as the other adults chuckled. I was puzzled.

When I left Italy in August of 1972, the country was very slowly becoming more multicultural with many Somali and Ethiopian students coming to Rome to enroll in the university. Some were friends, and they were Somali and Ethiopian to me. So it was a distinct process to learn that, even if I didn't see myself as white, I was seen as white with the tremendous accompanying social and historical meanings associated with that.

Aside from putting the return address on the back of an envelope, as opposed to the front, holding the fork on my left hand even though I am right-handed, and wondering if *honor* and *neighbor* should be spelled *honour* and *neighbour,* there are other non-American parts to me.

I am inevitably drawn to immigrants from anywhere. "Where are you from? How long have you been here?"—even when the questions raise caution in the person's eyes, "Why does she want to know this?" And if their native language is one I know, I can't help switching, "*Ah, vous êtes francophone?*" "*Entonces habla español?*" to learn more.

But as my genealogy clearly tells me, I am deeply American. John Kininmont in 1654, Robert Lucas in 1679—122 and 97 years, respectively, before 1776—and ancestors who fought in the Revolutionary War and for the Union. I shouldn't be surprised since the evidence is very clear, but the research has shown me just how deep this American part of my identity is. I am proud of it; I have come to own it.

I have very happily traveled and learned America since 1972 while keeping my eye on the door and on the world map on the wall. I remain an inveterate traveler; I feel nostalgic about places I have never even been to.

EPILOGUE

I CAME PRETTY CLOSE TO BECOMING THE DIALECT GEOGRAPHER that I told my mother I wanted to be. My academic training led to a faculty position in the Department of Linguistics at Gallaudet University, the world's only liberal arts university for deaf and hard-of-hearing people. I learned American Sign Language (ASL) on the job and stayed for thirty-one years with research focusing on the structure and use of sign languages, in particular regional and social variation—so, dialect geography. In retirement, I edit a scholarly journal about sign language research, *Sign Language Studies*, and still teach Italian to adults. I am a lifelong multilingual and have harbored a silent fear since 1973, after I left Italy and began teaching Italian, that the right side of my body would simply fall off if I stopped teaching it. So I continue. I was bilingual in Spanish and French first, but teaching seems to keep my body intact, along with periodically speaking and studying French and Spanish, studying spoken Irish since 1993, and continuing to use ASL now as a fledgling interpreter.

Researching and writing this memoir has been like standing on a very high hill looking out over a vast plain of family history. To the left, I look over New Mexico, Oklahoma, Indiana, and Pennsylvania, and Dunfermline, Fife, Longbridge Deverill, and Kent. Some of these are in the far distance, but they are firmly within my sights. Three hundred sixty-one years for the Kinnamans in the United States, ten generations; 336 years for the Lucas line, also ten generations. To the right, I see Guatemala, Italy, Phoenix, Walla Walla. I stand in the middle with the job of bringing both landscapes together into one narrative.

And the landscape to the right is not enough. It is one thing to simply say, "Oh, my family came from England" or "Yeah, my ancestors were Scots," with very broad brushstrokes. It is quite another to get into the fine details, as much as they are available—Robert Lucas who wanted the Indians in Delaware "cleered," the Oklahoma Land Rush, a saloon in Duran, New Mexico, presidential funerals in Guatemala . . . With the knowledge of my ancestors' stories, my memory now stretches back to sixteenth-century England. My understanding of how I got here doesn't just start in Phoenix in 1951; it starts in Kent, England, in 1500 and in Fife in the thirteenth century. That knowledge doesn't go away, and it completely shapes how I think of myself and my life. And learning about ancestors who got here in 1654 and 1679 eventually gets you to American history—the Revolutionary War, the Civil War, World Wars I and II, the Depression. With my eye on 1654 and 1679, I have backed into American history, which I had only a tenuous grasp on before I started researching my folks.

It strikes me that these are stories of white men of varying means going to foreign places to make their way with an ambiguous or downright hostile relationship with the humans who were already there—a thoroughly American story from Jamestown and Plymouth forward. One dilemma for my parents was that I seem to have consistently missed the point that I was an outsider. Both in Guatemala and Italy, I "went native"; I lost sight of the mission. My understanding was that I had been brought to live in Guatemala and Italy and that was my job: to learn the language, to enter the culture, both as far and as much as I possibly could. I always understood my role to be that of a full participant, no matter where I was.

Of course, the immigrants Robert Lucas and John Kininmont eventually did the same. And I certainly was not alone. Many children like me learned the respective languages and cultures they found themselves in and have kept that knowledge throughout their lives. Certainly not all—the children whose parents worked on the various American military bases in Italy like Livorno, Vicenza, Naples learned Italian hardly at all and had few Italian friends. But many of us did.

As I said in the prologue, the memories recounted here have hundreds of siblings. Thinking of all of them makes me imagine other possible lives. I could have found my way back to Guatemala and Latin America and made a life there; as did some of my classmates, I could have returned to Italy and Europe after college and lived my life there. I have made my life in America, incorporating frequent contact with Latin America, Europe, and other parts of the world, and it has been very rich. Writing the memoir has also left me with many questions for my parents, which will have to remain unanswered.

The question arises as to where home is. Isabel Allende provided a simple answer. A caller to the *Diane Rehm Show* in January of 2014—a woman from Colombia—said that she lives in the United States and is perplexed as to where home is—the United States or Colombia. Said Isabel Allende, "Your home is your memory, what you remember—the territory of memory."

That is a very familiar home to me, and my passport and visa are always current for that territory.

Acknowledgements

I OWE A SIGNIFICANT DEBT OF GRATITUDE to several people: Susan Moger, in whose Autobiographical Writing class at Anne Arundel Community College (Maryland) I started seriously shaping this memoir in the fall of 2013. She provided unfailing encouragement and helpful feedback all through the process of putting it together; she also prepared an earlier version of the manuscript for publication, for which I am grateful; my long-time colleague Deborah Tannen for her support of the publishing process; my colleagues at Gallaudet University—Ivey Wallace, director, GU Press, and Patrick Harris, chief engineer, Video Services, for their assistance and advice and especially Deirdre Mullervy, managing editor, GU Press, who prepared the final manuscript; Gary Gore, who designed the cover and prepared the images for publication; Sheryn Hara and her team at Book Publishers Network—Julie Scandora, Melissa Coffman, Scott Book and Erik Korhel; and Stephen Brown, my wonderful life partner, who has listened very patiently to all the stories and supported the development of the memoir. My gratitude also to Franklin, Kathleen et al.

For the "Carlos and Miguel" in "The Guatemala Years," I relied on the work of Stephen Streeter, Richard Immerman, and Nick Cullather. All three generously responded to email queries and phone calls, and Stephen Streeter took the time to read a draft of this section and send me very valuable feedback. My classmate from 1956–1960 at the Colegio Evelyn Rogers in Guatemala City, Bobby Rogers, took the school over from his mother and has been its director since 1989. He and Roberto Córdova, historian at the Guatemala National Archives, very generously helped me secure the newspaper photos in "Carlos and Miguel," along with the permission to use them.

For "Bert's Side," I am grateful to Helen Griffith and Lisa McQuillen of the library of Friends House London and to Robert Adam for helping procure a key article on Quakers in Wiltshire. Margaret Moles, Robert Jago, and Gill Neal of the Wiltshire Council and the Wiltshire and Swindon History Centre provided excellent information. Susan K. Forbes of the Kansas Historical Society, Tina Ortega and Okami Takiguchi of the Torrance County (New Mexico) Historical Society and Museum, and Jon May of the Oklahoma Historical Society sent key newspaper and journal articles and images. The staff at the Library of Congress Reading Room in Washington, DC, and Ancestry.com were very helpful, as were Alan Makey, Kristin Slater, and Michael Lucas of the Kent (England) Family History Society. Jane Hurst provided the map of the Lucas property in Delaware.

For "Kathleen's Side," I am deeply indebted to my relative Matt Kinnamont for his work on our family history. He provided the map of the Kinninmont property in Maryland, as well references for John Kinninmont's baptismal record and the record of transported prisoners. He also took the time to read a draft of this section and send me valuable feedback. Both of us are grateful to another relative, Lester Kinnamon, who did earlier work on our family. I am also grateful to David Dobson, a scholar of Scottish history and immigration, for his generous email communications. I am grateful to the staff of the Maryland Room of the Talbot County Free Library in Easton, Maryland. In particular, Monique Gordy led me to Matt Kinnamont and his work.

For "Italy," my 1960s classmate Doug Ritter provided an account of the founding of the Overseas School of Rome. I am grateful for my communications with him during the writing process.

For "1530/Home Leave," I am grateful to David Modeer and Crystal Thompson of the Central Arizona Project (CAP) and Ileen Snoddy of the Salt River Project for the valuable information they provided for this section.

Sources

Epigraph

Rubin, Louis, Jr. *Small Craft Advisory.* New York: The Atlantic Monthly Press, 1991.

Thomas, Dylan. *Reminiscences from Childhood.* BBC radio broadcast, 1943.

Guatemala

Cullather, Nick. *Secret History: The C.I.A.'s Classified Account of Its Operations in Guatemala.* Stanford, CA: Stanford University Press, 1999.

Immerman, Richard H. T*he CIA in Guatemala: The Foreign Policy of Intervention.* Austin, TX: University of Texas Press, 1982.

Streeter, Stephen M. *Managing the Counterrevolution—The United States and Guatemala, 1954–1961.* Columbus, OH: Center for International Studies, 2000.

Bert's Side

Battle, J. H. *History of Bucks County, Pennsylvania.* Cambridge: Cambridge Scholars Publishing, (1887) 2009.

Charles II, 1662. *An Act for preventing the Mischeifs and Dangers that may arise by certaine Persons called Quakers and others refusing to take lawfull Oaths. Statutes of the Realm: Volume 5, 1628-80.* Originally published by Great Britain Record Commission, s.l, 1819.

Davis, William H. *A Genealogical and Personal History of Bucks County.* Baltimore: Genealogical Publishing Company, 1975.

Elk City Enterprise (Kansas), September 23, 1893, 5.

http://genforum.genealogy.com/quaker/messages/2936.html, short article on Edward Lucas.

Hall, Betty Porter. *Governor Robert Lucas, his Ancestors and Descendants.* La Verne, CA: University of La Verne Press, 1989.

Hinshaw, W. *Encyclopedia of American Quaker Genealogy.* Baltimore, MD: Genealogical Publishing Company, 1969.

Ingle, H. Larry. *First among Friends: George Fox and the Creation of Quakerism.* Oxford: Oxford University Press, 1996.

Lucas, Robert (as told to Lucille Gilstrap). Homesteading the Strip. Chronicles of Oklahoma. *Quarterly of the Oklahoma Historical Society.* Oklahoma City. Volume LI (1991): 285–304.

Morning Reporter, Independence, Kansas, April 24, 1889, 1.

Pennsylvania Historical and Museum Commission (PHMC) Copied Survey Books, D-68, 124. Bureau of Archives and History, Pennsylvania State Archives.

Powell, W. R. The Society of Friends in Wiltshire. *Journal of the Friends Historical Society*, Vol. 44, No. 1 (1952): 3–10.

Prucha, Francis Paul. *America Indian Policy in the Formative Years: The Indian Trade and Intercourse Acts 1790–1834.* University of Nebraska Press, 1970.

Smith, Toby. "Arrows from Strong Bows." *New Mexico* magazine (February 1982): 20–27.

Tepper, Michael, ed. *Emigrants to Pennsylvania, 1641–1819. A consolidation of passenger lists from the Pennsylvania Magazine of History and Biography.* Baltimore, MD: Genealogical Publishing Company, 1975.

Whitehead, William A., and William Nelson, eds. *Documents Relating to the Colonial History of the State of New Jersey, Volume I. 1631–1687*, Daily Journal Establishment, Newark, 1880.

Wiltshire Council. http://history.wiltshire.gov.uk/community/getcom.php.

Kathleen's Side

Kinnamon, Lester. C. *The Kinnamon Family in America.* Talbot County, MD: privately printed, 1984.

Kinnamont, K. Matthew. *The Kinnamonts of the Eastern Shore of Maryland and the District of Columbia*. Master's Thesis, San Jose State University, 1996.

MacLean, Maggie. "Slavery in Maryland." History of American Wormen. July 7, 2008. Accessed April 4, 2017, www.womenhistoryblog.com.

Magnusson, Magnus. *Scotland—The Story of a Nation*. New York: Grove Press, 2000.

Stevenson, David. "Cromwell, Scotland and Ireland." In *Oliver Cromwell and the English Revolution*, edited by John Morrill, 155. Longman Group,1990.

Withers, Charles. *Gaelic in Scotland, 1698–1981*. Edinburgh: John Donald Publishers, 1984.

The Italy Years

Adams, William Lee. "Mind Your Manners: The Secret of Switzerland's Last Traditional Finishing School." *Time*, Monday, October 31, 2011.

Dickie, John. *Blood Brotherhoods—A History of Italy's Three Mafias*. New York: Public Affairs, 2011.

Encyclopedia Britannica Online, https://www.britannica.com/place/Italy/The-economic-miracle.

Ginzburg, Natalia. *Lessico Famigliare*. Arnoldo Mondadori Editore, 1971.

Hearder, H., and D. P. Walcy, eds. *A Short History of Italy*. Cambridge: Cambridge University Press, 1963.

Macadam, Alta. *Rome and environs (Blue Guide)*. New York: WW Norton, 1994.

OASR.org.

Ritter, Douglas. *La Dolce Vita: An American Childhood in Rome in the '60's*. Lulu Press, 2010.

Smith, Denis Mack. *Modern Italy: A Political History*. Ann Arbor, MI: University of Michigan Press, 1997.

Society of Dance History Scholars online. https://sdhs.org/barbara-sparti, retrieved March 11, 2015.

Stern, Michael. *An American in Rome*. Bernard Geiss Associates, 1964.

Vickers, Hugh. *Great Operatic Disasters*. New York: St. Martin's Griffin, 1979.